Sue Cranmer
Oct 2017

Collection of papers   Review by end March
2018

define AT

rich

accounts v. nuanced
    detailed

vast amounts of res of diff
    aspects of AT use

Accessibly written

Provides useful 'intro' to main aspects
    of field, ie disabs st, inclusion,
Identity, intersectionality

(through rich collection of papers)

concepts
    approaches.
Comes from disabs
field, quite different to
books on tech that
    emanate from tech studies.
(perspective)

NB Book - if you talk of
ATs in book, need to define
carefully as they're much
wider than just educ type
ie braille notetaker vs
    adapted bike / ski seat thingy

Book also discuss range of conceptual thinks,
ie p48 intro me to model of inclusion

Disability, Society and Assistive Technology

The provision of assistive technology is an important individual and collective service of the welfare state. The state plays a significant role towards linking users and products, and the matching of devices and users is both a science and an art. However, many people feel it is stigmatising to use individually designed assistive technologies as they often, in a subtle way, convey discriminating barriers in society. The major challenges of assistive technology are thus to reduce social exclusion and marginalisation and, importantly, to reduce individual risks and societal costs related to non-use due to deficiencies in usability, aesthetics and design of the technologies.

This groundbreaking book discusses the relationships among society, disability and technology by using different empirical examples (e.g., school, everyday life) to show why the combination of disability studies and STS-studies (science, technology and society) is a fruitful approach to understanding and meeting these challenges. The book explores the significance of the technologies for users, society and the field; identifies challenges to designing, adopting and using assistive technologies; and points at theoretical challenges in research as well as professional challenges in assistive technology service provision. The book also scrutinises the role of assistive technology devices, as well as the organisational structure of the assistive technology market, in relation to disabled people's lives.

This book will be valuable reading for students, academics, teachers and social educators interested in Disability Studies, STS Studies, Product Design, Sociology, Occupational Therapy and Physiotherapy, as well as engineers working in the field of assistive technology.

Bodil Ravneberg is a Professor at Western Norway University of Applied Sciences (HVL).

Sylvia Söderström is a Professor at the Faculty of Medicine and Health Science at The Norwegian University of Science and Technology (NTNU), Trondheim, Norway.

Interdisciplinary Disability Studies
Series editor: Mark Sherry
The University of Toledo, USA

Disability studies has made great strides in exploring power and the body. This series extends the interdisciplinary dialogue between disability studies and other fields by asking how disability studies can influence a particular field. It will show how a deep engagement with disability studies changes our understanding of the following fields: sociology, literary studies, gender studies, bioethics, social work, law, education, or history. This ground-breaking series identifies both the practical and theoretical implications of such an interdisciplinary dialogue and challenges people in disability studies as well as other disciplinary fields to critically reflect on their professional praxis in terms of theory, practice, and methods.

For a full list of titles in this series, please visit www.routledge.com/series/ ASHSER1401

Forthcoming

Child Pain, Migraine and Invisible Disability
Susan Honeyman

Disability and Art History
Edited by Elizabeth Howie and Ann Millett-Gallant

Organizing the Blind
The Case of ONCE in Spain
Roberto Garvía

Disability and Social Media
Global Perspectives
Edited by Mike Kent and Katie Ellis

Visual Impairment and Work
Experiences of Visually Impaired People
Sally French

Disability and Rurality
Identity, Gender and Belonging
Karen Soldatic and Kelley Johnson

Disability, Society and Assistive Technology

**Bodil Ravneberg and
Sylvia Söderström**

LONDON AND NEW YORK

First published 2017
by Routledge
2 Park Square, Milton Park, Abingdon, Oxon OX14 4RN

and by Routledge
711 Third Avenue, New York, NY 10017

Routledge is an imprint of the Taylor & Francis Group, an informa business

British Library Cataloguing-in-Publication Data
A catalogue record for this book is available from the British Library

Library of Congress Cataloging-in-Publication Data
Names: Ravneberg, Bodil, author. | Söderström, Sylvia, author.
Title: Disability, society, and assistive technology / Bodil Ravneberg and
    Sylvia Sèoderstrèom.
Other titles: Interdisciplinary disability studies.
Description: Abingdon, Oxon ; New York, NY : Routledge, 2017. |
    Series: Interdisciplinary disability studies | Includes bibliographical
    references and index.
Identifiers: LCCN 2016046306 | ISBN 9781472467652 (hardback) |
    ISBN 9781315570556 (ebook)
Subjects: MESH: Disabled Persons | Self–Help Devices | Biomedical
    Enhancement | Mainstreaming (Education) | Sociological Factors |
    Social Perception
Classification: LCC HV1568 | NLM HV 1568 | DDC 362.4—dc23
LC record available at https://lccn.loc.gov/2016046306

ISBN: 978-1-4724-4718-0 (hbk)
ISBN: 978-1-315-57742-5 (ebk)

Typeset in Times New Roman
by Apex CoVantage, LLC

MIX
Paper from
responsible sources
FSC
www.fsc.org FSC® C013604

Printed and bound by CPI Group (UK) Ltd, Croydon, CR0 4YY

Contents

1 Disability, society and assistive technology

A multidisciplinary field

How do we understand tech?

Whether in the home, at school, at work or at play, technology plays an important role in the lives of disabled people; it influences how people think about disability, their experiences with disability and how disability is framed in the society. We all have experiences with technology and probably also with some kind of assistive technology (AT), irrespective of whether or not we use AT. Most of us have family members, colleagues or friends who use AT. They are seldom indifferent to the use of devices. Even when it comes down to the smallest knots, screws and nuts, technical devices are loaded with feelings, meanings, traditions, cultural values and symbols (Woods and Watson 2004a).

What is AT, and what does it do? To investigate AT, we need a multidisciplinary approach that can grasp the complicated relationships among humans, technology and society. This book is a contribution in this direction. Our suggestion is to combine perspectives of disability studies with STS (science, technology and society) studies in order to grasp the complexity of AT. Thus, our contribution applies an approach to the field of AT that combines important perspectives from both disability and STS studies. *Like my phd.*

During the last decades, peoples' methods of communication and interaction have developed and changed contemporaneously as technology progresses. Technologies have become a vitally important aspect of people's lives, and their usage has evolved to confirm and underline identities and values, making technology and society mutually constitutive (MacKenzie and Wajcman 2005; Räsänen 2008). Postmodern social life is characterised by a domestication of technology, by individual choices, multiple identities and mobility. However, the characteristics that mark the lives of most people in Western societies are not so apparent in the lives of disabled people. In this book the relations among society, disability and AT is under scrutiny. In our investigation we also draw on empirical examples from disabled people's everyday life. We argue for the need of a new research approach combining the perspectives of disability studies and STS studies. In this introduction, we provide a short insight into our position at the intersection of the fields of disability studies, STS studies and AT. At the conclusion of the introduction, we give a short overview of the book.

This is what I'm also bringing tog. 1 bund umbrella of inclusion.

Humans + tech + society!

Our point of departure

Science is interpretation of data, and the scientist's background, perspective or point of departure affects how data are interpreted. Consequently, it is of vital importance to make relevant prerequisites and contexts transparent. Our point of initial departure is as researchers in the field of social sciences and disability studies. Our epistemological standpoint is rooted in the philosophical position of heterogeneous constructivism. The term *heterogeneous* refers to the mixtures of social (human) and non-social (technical) elements in the construction process (Hess 1997). Unlike social constructivism, which focuses on the arrow of causality from context to content, this heterogeneous constructivism also examines the opposite direction of causality, whereby technology shapes and constitutes new forms of social relationships. We believe it is possible to think about science much the same way as in duck-rabbit gestalt drawings in which two interpretations are simultaneously consistent with the material. This perspective also coincides with our point of departure in the field of Nordic disability studies.

Disability studies

Disability has been and continues to be perceived and experienced differently. Different professions study the subject differently, and within varying fields and contexts. Traditionally the field of medicine has dominated the way we understand disability, by adopting an understanding of disability as an individual characteristic, focusing on medical aspects of the body. From a disability studies' perspective the argument is that the provision of AT has been dominated by the medical model applying a 'clinical' touch or a 'one size-fits-all' approach. This is the case in many countries, such as in the UK. This is opposed to a social or a cultural model of understanding disability that applies an aesthetic and tailor-made design (Sapey, Stewart and Donaldson 2004).

Moreover, many researchers in disability studies have tried to move disability out of the realm of medicine (Oliver 1990; Garland-Thomson 1997; Breivik 2005). This research approach has been an important step towards a shift in how disability is conceived. Disability has, according to Rosemarie Garland-Thomson, 'been recast from a form of pathology or a lack, to societal barriers, attitudes and minority issues' (Garland-Thomson 1997:6). This perspective has shown to be fruitful, especially when it comes to the identities of deaf people (Breivik 2005) and can also be useful when it comes to AT if we consider the users not as a homogenous group, but as a landscape of minorities with different and fluid identities. Thus, we conceptualise disability as a social construction and relational phenomenon that takes place in interpersonal relationships, in encounters between humans and environments and between individuals and society (Gustavsson, Tøssebro and Traustadottir 2005). Consequently, it is not a person's impairment that governs their use of AT, but rather the social practices in which this use takes place.

Social scientists and disability studies scholars have paid much attention to individual needs, equality and societal barriers, but have not dwelled much on the technological side of the disability concept. This book is a contribution to this side of the disability concept without ignoring previously important contributions provided by disability scholars such as Karp (1998), Lupton and Seymour (2000) and Woods and Watson (2004). STS scholars have also picked up some aspects of the technological side of the disability concept, but surprisingly little work has been done. Important contributions, however, have been made by Moser and Law (1998), Moser (2003), Rose and Blume (2003), Anderberg (2006), Winance (2006), Olaussen (2010), Galis (2011) and Blume, Galis and Pineda (2014). Our purpose in combining the complex fields of disability studies and STS studies is to add to the understanding of the (dis)abling effects of materiality throughout the life course.

Such (dis)abling effects of materiality may include the significance of socio-material practices in children's everyday school life. These socio-material practices facilitate disabled children's participation when AT is used intentionally. It turns out, however, that every small inattentive moment rapidly places them in social isolation. Other effects of this materiality are the importance of assistive Information and Communication Technology (ICT) for young people's social life, illuminating emerging differentiation through social anticipations and technological shortcomings.

Effects of materiality also influence disabled people's possibilities for participation in leisure activities; in this book, this influence illuminated by elderly people's use of stair lifts in their home in order to save energy to do physical exercises, or disabled children's participation in leisure activities. The (dis)abling effects of materiality are furthermore evident in the processes of acquiring AT, adapting and individualising AT, and integrating AT into workplaces, private homes and caregiving. Caregiving, especially for the elderly, is changing due to demographic changes, involving an ideology called 'ageing in place'. To achieve ageing in place, advanced assistive technologies are installed in elderly people's homes and at service providers. Such technologies are supposed to help individuals perform actions, such as a stair-lift may do, to prevent or identify threatening situations, such as an alarm or a sensor may do, even though they may also limit actions, such as a navigation device (for instance a GPS) or a lock may do. The intention of these technological implementations is to provide effective and sound services, enhancing the recipients' independent living. However, many of the new technological solutions are still fragmented and not user-friendly enough, and the effects have so far been little documented (Devik and Hellzen 2012; Dugstad et al. 2015).

Even though disabled people are just as different and diverse as non-disabled people are, they seem to share some vital perceptions of usable AT as technologies that symbolize enhancement, capabilities and identities. They can also function as representations of identities, such as age, lifestyle or gender. Many AT users perceive their AT devices as important body parts, whether the device is a wheelchair or a hearing aid. Usability, design and aesthetics turn out to be important dimensions of AT, whether the users have a physical, sensory or cognitive impairment.

Approaches to tech

STS studies

STS studies represents an anti-positivist approach to science and technology. Rather than conceiving of techno-science as engaging in the practice of discerning facts about things apart from interest, justice and power, STS studies demonstrates that the knowledge of things, humans and power relations cannot be seen separate from one another (Olaussen 2010; Skjølsvold 2015).

An STS studies perspective emphasises that we first shape our technological products; subsequently, the technological devices shape us. This is because technological devices have *two* sides. They are both a consequence of and a prerequisite to social practices (Latour 1992; Gieryn 2002). Moreover, technologies shape action (Winance 2006) and identities (Akrich 1992; Oudshoorn, Saetnan and Lie 2002). This means that technical devices are actors in themselves. This perspective on technology facilitates a sharpened focus upon the crucial role of AT alongside human aid in, for example, (re)habilitation processes. The devices are not seen as neutral, nor are they taken for granted, neglected, or seen as finished or 'dead' products. More precisely, AT products, when seen as non-human actors, are *social constructions* that partake in the negotiation processes (Latour 1992; Berg 1994; Moser 2003; Winance 2006; Skjølsvold 2015). This contribution from STS studies brings life to the non-human actor and facilitates a scrutinised look at the relationships among AT, disability and society. In our investigation of these relationships, we find the actor-network perspective to be a most useful analytical tool.

An actor-network perspective

In the late 1980s, STS scholars acknowledged the need to develop analytical tools based on anti-essentialist attitudes towards science, technology and society. They asserted that science is a process in which the social, technical, conceptual and textual are puzzled together and transformed. Out of this development emerged the actor-network theory (ANT), which is not a theory at all, but rather an ethno-methodological approach to investigation.

Bruno Latour initiated ANT (1987). He claimed that objects, machines, technologies and humans are all equal parts in reciprocal networks of connections and joining actions, all actively influencing each other, and all being actors (Latour 2008). *Actors* generate effects. Thus, any object, artefact or person who generates an effect by making a difference is an actor. Actors may indicate, encourage, permit, influence, make possible, determine or obstruct actions. Therefore, who and what enter into an action, or a *social practice*, need to be carefully scrutinised. Human actions, communication and symbols only constitute one part of social practices; things, objects and technologies constitute the other part. In social practices, the connections and joining of actions create network effects that constitute *social structure.* Latour (2008) suggested that we should follow the actors, reveal their actions, and show how the social structure is created, thus clearly indicating that the ANT approach also focuses on societal issues and how society is produced (Skjølsvold 2015).

Our perception of disability is that disability is a phenomenon that is situated and contextual, and it occurs in practical and relational encounters. Thus, in order to investigate how this phenomenon emerges in ongoing social interactions and encounters, and simultaneously pay attention to the significance of the material dimensions in these interactions, we employ an ANT perspective. In the research field of disability studies an ANT perspective yields important insights not only into how AT makes the articulation of identity possible, but also into the interdependency between technology and person in this negotiation. Using ANT as an analytical tool, we take a closer look at how disability in our society is handled and understood by asking how actions, agency, influences and effects circulate and change (dis)ability over time. Things – the material – carry agency. It is thus essential to include the material dimension if we want to understand how science, technologies and societies are mounted or put together and how relations change (Skjølsvold 2015). What are the possibilities, what relations do these possibilities emerge from, what is done in practice and what effects does a technological solution or device bring for the person(s) in question? These conditions materialise in socio-material practices in which facts, objects and nature are not given nor taken for granted, but are effects of interactions, relations and orderings.

In addition to ANT's inclusion of artefacts and technologies as actors which effect interactions, this perspective's advantage before other constructivist perspectives is that ANT focuses on how alterations in socio-material practices are made. Such socio-material practices may include how disabled people use their AT, how AT influence the possibilities of actions and interactions, and how these possibilities affect the persons involved. This approach characterises our entrance into the fields of STS, disability and assistive technology. Seeing technologies as scripts as outlined in the following is part of this picture.

A disability script perspective

Donna Haraway (1991:164) contends that technologies are 'crucial tools recrafting our bodies' and 'enforcing new social relations' between people. From this perspective machines such as computers, mobile telephones, glasses, wheelchairs and hearing instruments are all 'prosthetic devices', 'intimate components' or 'friendly selves', as Haraway describes them (1991:169). A definition of a cyborg is an organism that adds to or enhances its abilities by using technology. An important aspect of the cyborg image at stake here is that this image offers people an environment or a terrain in which to negotiate identities and construe new self-understandings. The cyborg image deals with identity. It enables creativity and self-representation in the process of developing the relationship between humanity and technology. From this perspective glasses, hearing instruments, wheelchairs and other technical devices are important, reconstituting not only embodiment, but also skill, gender and sexuality.

In the eyes of many disabled people and certainly in the eyes of Deaf people, ATs 'are mundane, everyday instruments in much the same way the hearing regard their telephones, TV sets, alarm clocks and doorbells' (Wendell 1996:29). However,

AT devices are special. Their design is for disabled users, and they are not easy to buy in the ordinary market. The products say a lot both implicitly and explicitly about disability and contemporary views on disability. Thus, AT devices may be analysed as 'disability scripts' (Olaussen 2010). Analyses of AT devices tell stories about disability. Inscribed into the devices and the cultural integration process are different norms and values about disability. This perspective on disability and technology can add to our understanding of how AT devices and their designs can hinder or encourage activities, actions and mobility related to identity, gender and disability.

The gender script perspective

The gender script perspective connects closely to the constructivist approach of perceiving artefacts within the STS studies approach. Built into devices and artefacts are norms about gender, but people rarely reflect much about this in everyday life (Akrich 1992; Oudshoorn et al. 2002). Often we see artefacts as genderless, as neutral, or we accept them at face value as masculine or feminine artefacts. A gender script approach states that devices always have reflections about gender built into them. Manufacturers that make innovative products inscribe a special view of the world and its users into the technology. There are different ways to interpret these reflections, as in user instructions, advertising, symbolism or division of labour (Akrich 1992). Technologies that surround us (personal computers, mobile phones, robots, bicycles and cars) reveal a lot about norms and values with regard to identity, such as gender or age. Innovators or designers anticipate the users' preferences, motives, tastes and skills. Through this, they might utilise gender devices and relate design of technologies to cultural norms.

The gender script perspective emphasises the importance of the use of the technology. Users are important contributors in the construction and formation processes of technology. The gender script approach emphasises the use of the technologies more than the production of them as a knowledge source (Berg 1994).The French philosopher Michel Foucault might have claimed that technologies are archaeological artefacts with layers of knowledge built into the design. The devices thus speak an implicit language that says something about what producers had in mind when they planned and produced new technologies, and it tells something about anticipated needs. Technologies can be read as a book, describing how designers anticipate their use and by whom. An interesting question is then, 'How might we investigate encounters and relationships among technology, disability, gender and other emergent categories?' In our quest for a better understanding of these dynamic and interactive phenomena, we add an intersectional perspective to our investigation.

An intersectionality perspective

Intersectionality has particular relevance for research with individuals who encounter multiple forms of oppression (Stirrat, Meyer, Oulette and Gara 2008). It proposes that one single identity category, such as disabled, cannot be used as the only analytical frame without exploring how issues of other identity categories additionally come to bear on the person's experience as disabled. The challenge is to understand and analyse a person as multidimensional, yet uniquely whole (Samuels and Ross-Sheriff 2008).

An intersectional perspective provides the opportunity to reveal new patterns and to demonstrate how new categories and identities emerge (Reyes de los and Mulinari 2005). This perspective focuses on the results of globalisation and individualisation, through the analysis of identity markers, social structures and power relations. An intersectional perspective links together the individual, the institutional and the structural levels. An example of this is when a disabled person presents him/herself as an ordinary person in the peer group, but is prevented from participating in ordinary settings due to institutional resources or might even be segregated from valued settings due to societal regulations.

An intersectional perspective points to fractures, highlights connections and deconstructs discourses. This perspective ties identity, power and inequality to individuals' possibilities to act as subjects within the frame of society's structures, institutional practices and prevailing ideologies. Intersectionality makes visible connections that consist of power and maintain inequality, and it involves highlighting the qualitatively different situations that emerge in the simultaneous effect of categories, such as age, gender and disability (Reyes and Mulinari 2005).

The intersectional perspective posits that a person's experiences reflect social constructions simultaneously, as these experiences have a relational aspect (Browne and Misra 2003). In this book, we focus on individual and relational aspects of identity, while also placing the individuals in their contemporary context, and anchor their actions in the prevailing ideologies and social structures. Thus, we find it appropriate to employ an intersectional perspective in this book on disability, society and AT.

Assistive technology

Assistive technology (AT) may be defined as any item, piece of equipment or product that is applied to secure, increase, maintain or improve functional capabilities (Wielandt, McKenna, Tooth and Strong 2006). ATs are also technologies used to improve, expand or extend people's performances, actions and interactions, and thus they are often experienced as an extension of the body (Lupton and Seymour 2000; Moser 2006; Winance 2006). However, using assistive technologies involves more than overcoming environmental barriers; it also involves symbolic, historical and cultural contexts. AT is loaded with collective cultural traditions, symbols and values, and subjective feelings and meanings assigned to the technology (Pape, Kim and Weiner 2002; Wielandt et al. 2006).

ATs are devices, big or small, that make everyday life easier for people. Such technologies are prerequisites for living an independent life for many and are also connected to universal design. ATs integrate people into the community and open it up for participation; they enable creative shaping of self and social identities. AT devices or products deal with functional (dis)abilities stemming from injuries, illnesses, losses, bodily weariness or accidents, temporarily or permanently. AT is supposed to support people (and their helpers/service providers) in performing various practical tasks in daily life. For instance, alarm devices serve many different purposes and come in many different shapes and forms. They signal, detect or warn that it is time to get up, that there is a fire or a burglar in your house or that someone is at the door or on the phone. The devices have a central position in the building. The devices attract the users' attention by vibrating, flashing or blinking.

Use of assistive technology

Using AT is symbolically, culturally and historically contextualised. In this respect, AT promotes but also *impedes* social participation. It can even be a hindrance for people. Thus, AT is not valued the same way as other possessions; in fact, assistive devices are much more contested (Watson 2002; Scherer 2005; Pullin 2009; Olaussen 2010). Take, for instance, the cochlear implant. Many deaf people, who view themselves as belonging to a cultural and linguistic minority, reject the device (Breivik 2005). They see it as another symbol of the medicalised perception of deafness forcing oral language upon them, causing them suffering as in the past (Blume 1999).

Devices have been abandoned by users for several reasons. Many devices end up in drawers or cupboards. This is, of course, not efficient for users, for public services or for the national health economy. Moreover, it could even be (very) risky or hazardous for the individual. What are the reasons for this abandonment? One answer is that users may feel stigmatised by the design of the technology (Pape et al. 2002; Wielandt et al. 2006; Söderström and Ytterhus 2010). It does not fit with their identity (as the cochlear implant exemplifies). We need to take into account that ATs are identity markers with a dual or a double-edged nature: a tool for independence on the one side, but also a symbol of disability or dependence on the other (Scherer 2005; Söderström and Ytterhus 2010).

Abandonment of devices may also be due to many other reasons. The list is long and may include lack of access to AT, lack of information about devices, repair and maintenance, professional powers, changes in the user's functional abilities or activities, inflexibility or ineffective device performance, lack of support, lack of motivation, minimal or no need for the device, negative family attitudes and so on (Scherer 2002; Pullin 2009; Söderström and Ytterhus 2010; Prior 2011, Ravneberg 2012). What happens when devices are abandoned and do not facilitate action and participation? As we shall see, there are different strategies among assistive technology users, and they manage and cope with this situation differently.

It is our argument that up to now AT and its importance to people has been a neglected issue in social sciences. Traditionally, research in the field has been, and still is, very technical or therapeutic in nature, as engineers have primarily focussed more on functionalities and utilities than on design or usability, and therapists have focussed on treatment and rehabilitation. Sociologists and political scientists have not done much research in this field, and there has been minimal research that focuses on users as participants or as subjects, rather than objects, in the AT market. In this book, we particularly highlight perspectives that present AT users as subjects and participants.

Assistive technology and (re)habilitation

Assistive technology also deals with important (re)habilitation issues. In this way, these technologies connect to the medical discourse. Since the first half of the twentieth century, many or most AT products have been produced as medical products and distributed as such (Woods and Watson 2004a). Using a wheeled chair in its formative period was interpreted as a sign that medicine had failed to find a cure or that the wheelchair user had given up on rehabilitation (Woods and Watson 2004a). Hearing aids had a similar history, with close connections to medicine. As a symbol of disability, hearing instruments have been associated with old age or mental deficiency.

A new (re)habilitation paradigm is in operation today, however. This paradigm puts more attention on how to change built and attitudinal features of environments that impede people's participation. This new paradigm pays less attention to the limitations of disability and gives more credence to universal design (Scherer 2005). This paradigm became more important when the UN Convention on the Rights of Persons with Disabilities (CRPD) was signed by many countries in 2008. The British social model has been influential in this respect, as it, more than others, has challenged the medical conceptions of disability (Shakespeare 2006). The social model aims at reducing social and physical barriers that exclude people from participating in the main stream of social activities (Oliver 1990). The British approach to understanding disability also uses *disabled people* as its main term (as is also the case in this book), meaning that disability is not something that people have, as the term *people with disabilities* indicates. Disability is instead something done to people with impairments; they are being hindered by, for instance, inaccessible public places, inaccessible transport systems or the unwelcoming attitudes by others.

Universal design

Furthermore, assistive technologies connect to universal design (UD). UD has become more and more important to implement during the last decades in order to make cities, buildings, transport, spaces, facilities and ICT more accessible to all people. The relationship between disability and UD, however, is a complex person-environment interplay (Lid 2014). It is also difficult to draw the line between universal design and individual design.

Accessible public spaces and environments, free of obstacles, are important for all, including disabled people. UD, however, is not designed closely for the individual as a 'design for me' AT. Rather, UD is positioned in the surroundings as a fixed or stationary 'design for all' technology. UD is thus a complicated matter and poses many challenges. One major challenge is that there is no standard individual accessing public places and environments, but a multitude of individuals with different abilities, wishes and personal standards. UD raises ethical questions as well as dilemmas of sameness and equality. The last can be illustrated by the dilemma of choosing between a stair-climbing chair and a ramp. The dilemma is whether disabled people should stress their sameness with everyone else in order to obtain access and equal rights, or stress their difference in order to have society respond to their special needs (Bickenbach 2014). Bickenbach (2014) and Winance (2014) argue that UD tends to ignore differences. This discussion of independence and power connected to UD and AT adds to the understanding of UD as a contested, 'wicked issue', as it illustrates how complicated it is to draw the line between 'design for me' and 'design for all'.

UD deals with different conflicts and should be discussed at all levels: at the societal level, when it comes to questions of ethics, human rights and democratic values; at the group level when it comes to technical standards; and at the individual level when it comes to usability, recognition, access and experiences (Lid 2013). It is important to emphasise that design priorities should not be either UD or individual design, but both. In order to make the best design priorities, it is important to get to know people's experiences in order to understand different (in) capacities, how they come about as well as the different facets of the interactions between people and the object or the environment they use (Winance 2014).

In the space between the individual and the environment there are different technologies positioned, all with agency and an aim to provide accessibility and usability for the individual. It is important to emphasise that such provisions, irrespective of whether they are universally designed or individual assistive technologies, need to be negotiated in order to be usable and stigma-free for the individual.

It is interesting to note, however, that many governments, including the Norwegian government, have recently made UD action plans in which they prioritize increased use of ICT-solutions and welfare technologies as important aspects of universal design. The Norwegian government states that 'people are surrounded by smart products and technologies that should be taken more advantage of, in order to improve everyday life for all' (Barne-, likestillings- og inkluderingsdept 2016). Here lies another challenge: People do not take enough advantage of all the technologies that are available. The aim for the governments is, for instance, to enable more students to follow teaching programs at schools or universities by requiring that educational institutions use and implement everyday life technologies and welfare technologies to a greater extent than they do now. UD action plans also include measures for other built environments, such as factories, plants, outdoor facilities, and transport, and encourage collaboration between and within municipalities and regions.

Provision of assistive technology and its market

Assistive technologies are different from other technologies or possessions that people might have. These are smart, special and exclusive devices. As such, they are difficult to obtain. In many countries, such technology is not available (Borg, Larsson and Östergren 2011). However, in many countries the provision of AT has become an important national responsibility and service, ensured by the welfare state. The state has come to play a significant role in linking users and products. Today the matching of devices and consumers actually has become a science and an art (Scherer 2002). Assistive technology is of great importance for users across identities for one major reason – they are very dependent upon it.

The provision of AT has to date taken place in restricted and regulated markets. Vendors, designers, producers and users take part in these markets based on certain conditions set by the state on behalf of the users. Countries differ with regard to the mixture of market and state provision of AT. In some countries, the AT market has become highly state regulated, as in Norway. In other countries, it is less regulated and more decentralised. In the United Kingdom, private actors are participating at a greater level compared with the Nordic countries. The development of AT services has been a slow evolution rather than a revolution in many Western countries.

If we look upon AT as a research field within the social sciences (sociology, political science and social economics) in particular, we may argue that not much attention has been paid to study the interactions among AT, humans and the society. A market approach to AT has also not yet been taken with regard to power structures. This is surprising given that the position of the user is very important in many markets. In fact, the more influential the user, the more his or her views will become materialised into the technical design of the new product (Akrich 1992). As we will see, users have had some impact on product development within the field of AT, but they have also been marginalised.

Wheelchair design has, however, advanced significantly. Since the 1990s much effort has brought attention to the person using the chair (Karp 1998). Hearing instruments have also undergone a technological revolution since the 1990s when they became digitalised. Moreover, the increasing permeability of analogue and digital technologies involves different challenges for different disabled people (Söderström 2009).

The perspectives of the book

A combination of the poly-theoretical lens of STS and disability studies facilitates analysis of the relationship between disability and technology without falling into the barriers of either the social or the medical model, thus cutting through them, so to speak (Schillmeier and Domenèch 2009). The perspective of this book is sociological *and* technological, seeing assistive technology as an object of human agency and as an independent agent. We shape our technological devices and afterwards they shape us. In order to understand the design, use and evaluation of technological devices, we have to look upon them as humanly constructed items. Design is both the planning of material things and the resolution of sometimes competing social interests. Powerful voices and their interests are etched into the artefact itself through the design process. Through the design processes, the enrolment of investors, patrons, consumers, managers, the eager public, regulators and vendors is accomplished. Often the shape of the product is to fit the wants and needs of those who must be committed to move it off the drawing board (Gieryn 2002).

In this book, AT is not limited to or only treated as devices that are helping people overcome environmental barriers; nor are the lived lives of people merely the context of assistive technology. AT is more than compensation for functional limitations. It consists of types of individual designs, representing personal identities and abilities. Hence, ATs are not 'dead' technical devices, but actors and identity markers in people's lives. Perceiving the mundane lives of people – women and men at all ages living different lives with different lifestyles – is equally important in understanding the integration of AT devices into their lives, at work, at school, in care or in their homes. Because of the identity approach used in this book, the focus is on devices' *usability* more than their utility or effectiveness. A definition of usability is user friendliness according to ISO 9241–11:

> The extent to which a product can be used by specified users to achieve specified goals with effectiveness (task completion by users), efficiency (task in time) and satisfaction (responded by user in term of experience) in a specified context of use.
>
> (Jokela, Livari, Maetro and Karukka 2003)

For public services, it is economically inefficient if devices are stuck in drawers or cupboards in people's homes. A lack of usability might be due to a missing link between users and designers or users' lack of power in this market. It can also be explained by demanding users, a lack of user orientation, insensitiveness within public services or a lack of acknowledgment or understanding about the crucial role that technology, in all its facets, plays in people's lives. In short, it is hard to find the right device for the right person.

A major challenge of AT from a societal perspective is how to reduce both individual risks and societal costs, as well as social exclusion and marginalisation. This book discusses the relationships among society, disability and technology by using different empirical examples. It argues that disability and STS studies offer a fruitful approach to understand and meet the challenges of AT by exploring the significance of the technologies for users, society and the field. Finally it identifies theoretical, empirical, and practical challenges.

Overview of the book

This introductory chapter discusses the field of AT and identifies why combining disability studies with STS perspectives is an effective method to gain a better understanding of a field consisting of different markets, users, service providers and practices. An important argument is that the design of AT devices not only deals with utility and functionality, but also with usability and human communication, and that AT acts as an identity marker for people.

Chapter 2 draws on a study comparing the quality of life of elderly people with impairments and/or chronic illnesses before and after the installation of a new technology – a stair lift – in their house or apartment. The relationship between the stair lift, human aid/services and different users is scrutinised. Important issues include how the technology effects the users' quality of life and their participation in social life, their need for formal and/or informal help and the possibility of their living longer in the home.

Chapter 3 is about participation in leisure activities. The chapter focuses on disabled children's experiences with AT in leisure-time activities. It draws on childhood sociology and perceives children as competent social actors. Examples are taken from studies on children's use of assistive activity technologies and participation in physical leisure activities. Even though this chapter is about disabled children and their experiences with assistive activity technologies in leisure activities, their experiences do not differ substantially from disabled adults' experiences in similar situations. Whether focusing on children, youth or adults, studies have shown that participation in sports and leisure activities contribute to enhanced relationships with peers, counter stigmatisation, redefine physical capabilities and provide a greater sense of control (Kissow and Singhammer 2012; Cook and Shinew 2014; Wilhite, Martin and Shank 2016).

These studies do not differentiate between different sporting and activity contexts. However, their findings do suggest that participating in sport and leisure activities is a vital site for disabled people, whether young or elderly, to explore the negotiation of identity, embodiment, social status and confidence. Children develop into youth and adults in relation to others and in the context of the broader society in which they live. Thus, we find disabled children's experiences with participation in leisure activities of special interest in illuminating how opportunities and barriers to inclusion in the local community emerge in early life.

Chapter 4 deals with the school system and the ways in which it constructs disability, including the consequences this has for inclusion and exclusion. This chapter discusses the significance of AT in school, specifically classroom practices, which show that the socio-material routines of the classroom put disabled pupils in a constantly flow in and out of participation and isolation.

Chapter 5 investigates the significance of assistive ICT as a tool in young disabled people's identity negotiations. To analyse the impact of assistive ICT, two different but closely related perspectives are used. The point of departure is that political policies in many countries aim at securing an information society for all, emphasising the importance of ICT and stressing that it can be used by everybody, including disabled people. The object of the chapter is to provide enhanced insight into the field of participation research by illuminating how assistive ICT is an actor that sometimes promotes and sometimes inhibits young disabled people's social participation. While the body of research on young people's use of ICT is quite comprehensive, research addressing digital differentiation in young people's use of ICT is still in its early stages.

Chapter 6 discusses the significance of aesthetics and design within AT, problematizing such variables as lifestyle, gender and age. The chapter argues that aesthetics and individual design are important to people's quality of life. It takes a closer look at AT and its use, or non-use, in everyday life, or the 'consumption junction'. The effort is to place the consumer in the centre of the network (at the consumption junction), viewing it inside out from his or her perspective. The focus is on what elements stand out as being more important than others for users and which paths they find wise to pursue.

Chapter 7 discusses signal devices and safety alarms and how this technology is integrated into routine life and work. This type of AT provides, as does mainstream ICT, important links between households and workplaces, individual users and the world beyond their front door. The chapter focuses on different barriers in the transaction phases of AT and how these barriers are met by users in the integration process.

Chapter 8 discusses principal questions regarding different actors in the market, such as public and private providers, users and users' families. This relates to the ambivalence between generosity and restrictiveness in the welfare state, the 'free play' of the market, and the user's legitimate or non-legitimate wishes and requests for (tailor-made) public services. The purpose of the chapter is to discuss these uncertainties and reveal tensions between the actors.

Chapter 9 discusses the relationship between assistive technologies and universal design, which are seen as two different but inter-connected approaches – 'design for me' vs. 'design for all'. The chapter addresses the complicated matter of drawing the line between the two approaches and argues that choice of solutions can be seen as negotiations on a societal, group and individual level, as the two approaches are not either-or solutions, but are placed on a continuum between universal solutions one the one end and targeted particularism on the other. The chapter also discusses the challenge of UD: that there exists no standard individual accessing public places and environments, but a multitude of individuals with different abilities, wishes and personal standards.

Chapter 10 addresses the theoretical, practical and social implications of the foregoing chapters. The chapter first presents a summary of the different arenas, perspectives and practices discussed throughout the book. Then a new multidisciplinary approach to the AT field is presented. The chapter draws a new picture of the AT field with its different mixtures of social and non-social elements, negotiation processes and power structures.

2   Assistive technologies, disability and elderly people

Technologies and quality of life

Because of longevity and normal physical deterioration, researchers have stated that old age has become a risk factor in itself in modern societies (Schillmeier and Domènech 2010; Walker and Foster 2013). This is close to saying that old age has become a disability. Historically, the cultural constructions of old age and disability have many similarities, thus making it complex to distinguish between illnesses connected to old age and those connected to disability. Types of impairments can just be part of the individual habitus or the trappings of old age. Old people are not necessarily disabled just because they have some sort of impairment (Priestly 2003). In this book, the approach is one that views old age as well as disability in terms of the identities of people themselves and how they are in the process of becoming elderly or aged. Being old is something you sometimes feel and other times forget, and it has less to do with actual age (Tulle-Winton 2002).

Today more and more elderly people live alone at home. Many are receiving little aid or are not receiving any help at all in case of illness, accident or mundane obstacles. This is why some have stated that old age has become a risk factor in itself. Elderly people and in particular disabled elderly people often need help. They face many types of difficult situations due to physical impairments. Sometimes no friends, neighbours or relatives are there to assist them, even in the case of an emergency. Demographic changes have transformed our societies, challenging both institutional and traditional solutions. Worries over ageism, exclusion or marginalisation of aged people have come to the fore. There are fears of undermining the generation contract or the ways in 'which goods and burdens ought to be shared in society between working-age cohorts and older generations' (Ervik and Lindén 2013:1). From a societal perspective, technological policies that give assistive technologies a major role as one of the answers to the demographic pressure have become urgently needed (Schillmeier and Domènech 2010). Engineers are developing new care technologies, such as personal care robots, as we speak, and research is being conducted on the impact new assistive-living technologies have on traditional caregiving, on the quality of life for elderly people at home, on institutional care, and so on. This shift has occurred alongside a new ideology called 'ageing in place,' as 'ageing in environments to which old people are accustomed is believed to enable them to remain more independent, despite growing frailty' (Roberts, Mort and Millingan 2002:19).

This chapter draws on a study comparing the quality of life of eight elderly people, women and men, with disabilities and/or chronic illnesses, before and after the installation of a new technology, a *stair lift,* in their house or apartment (Islam and Ravneberg 2009). The chapter describes changes in the relationships among private informal help, public formal help (human aid/services) and the users because of the new technology. Important issues are whether and how the stair lift enhances the quality of life and what effects it has on participation in social life, the need for formal and/or informal help and the possibility to be able to live longer at home.

Assistive technologies can be either fixed in the house, such as a stair lift, or portable/mobile, such as a safety alarm. They are supposed to help individuals perform actions, provide security or identify threatening situations. Telecare is one solution that helps individuals live independently by securing their safety. Technologies can also limit actions or relations in different ways. It is important to note that technologies are not only merely aid; they are also identity markers with a potential to stigmatise. Moreover, they can function as surveyors or monitors. People might conceive of them as coercive, protective or a negotiable combination of both (López 2010). The feeling of being stigmatised or surveyed might explain why some people refuse (if they can) to use certain technologies. In this way, technologies limit actions or relations. In this chapter, however, the focus is not on hindrances, but on how stair lifts help individuals to perform actions.

A study on the impact of stair lifts on people's lives

Stair lifts are an example of a fixed technology that requires housing adaptation in order to help people move between house floors or in and out of a building. Stair lifts are installed inside the house or in the staircase of a bigger building. The building constructors can also install it outside a building or a house, for instance from the house to a garden or to the street. Stair lifts can be very different from one another. Designers or building constructors build the stair lifts to suit the staircase in question. For example, some have curved tracks designed to suit staircases that turn corners or spiral. An installation of a stair lift might cause reactions from neighbours in a block of apartments if they see it as a negative intervention in the house.

The following is based on interviews in their homes with eight people between the ages of 59 and 85 years who had a stair lift (paid by the state) or who were eligible for one and waiting for it to be installed (at the time of the interview). They all lived at home, alone or with their spouse or family. They had different mobility impairments and some had developed chronic illnesses. At the time of the interview, six participants, three men and three women, had a stair lift installed in their house, while two women were waiting for one.

Important questions considered included: How did the users or their neighbours react to the installation of the stair lift? What impact do users think it has on their quality of life? What does their home mean to them as compared to the alternative of institutional care? Are there gender differences? What activities are important to them? Do they spend more time outside of the house because of the stair lift? What disabling barriers do they confront apart from the staircase? Does the technology alter the relationship between formal and informal care, and if so, how? Who uses the technology a little? Who uses it a great deal, and why? What follows is an analysis of the interviews, highlighting elements in their daily lives that had changed for all the informants after the installation, by way of using individual examples.

Active outdoors

To begin with, all the informants who lived in a block of flats or in housing cooperatives stated that none of their neighbours had reacted negatively to the installation of the lifts. One housing cooperative, however, did not want to alter the size of a garage (move the wall) so that a wheelchair could come through. The informant had to get a new, smaller and more expensive chair instead.

Brian, the youngest informant (59 years), is single and lives alone in an apartment on the third floor of a five-floor low-rise building without an elevator. He goes shopping and plays bingo more or less every day, travelling around using a wheelchair and buses. He has two electric outdoor wheelchairs as well as crutches, and an indoor working chair for the kitchen. Before the installation of the stair lift, he walked the stairs alone very, very slowly, holding the rail with the two crutches in his hand. Nevertheless, he went out every day: 'Yes, I had to get out, did I not?' The big difference for him after the installation is that it does not take as long to get up and down the stairs. The stair lift has helped him become more active outdoors. He is happy that he can manage his life more on his own. Most importantly, after the stair lift, he can live in his apartment for a much longer time, which is important to him.

The stair lift has not altered his need for formal or informal care or for help in the apartment. He still gets weekly help from his son. He also gets assistance from public services as before. The biggest change is that the staircase enables him to go out more than before. He can continue doing the shopping and cooking by himself. He is also able to maintain a social life, for instance, attending bingo evenings. With the stair lift, he has prolonged his preferences for what to do in his daily life, and when and how to do it. This is the greatest benefit to him. It is also the most cost-effective means for the society, as moving Brian to an institution would cost much more.

Energy saving

Ted is a 75-year-old married man. He lives with his wife on the fourth floor of a low-rise building. Before the stair lift, his wife helped him a lot, carrying stuff up the stairs, as he could not manage this on his own. Since the installation of the stair lift, daily life has improved for Ted and his wife, and her back pain has lessened. 'It has not so much to do with time saved, but with health saved,' Ted said of the stair lift. He got the stair lift at the same time as the Assistive Service Centre rebuilt his old car so that he can drive by himself, using his hands only.

He has no other assistive devices, except for a stick if he feels very unsteady when walking outdoors. Because of the lift and the rebuilding of the car, his life is well-functioning, and according to Ted, his quality of life has improved. However, he does not use the stair lift every time he goes out. He uses it primarily when he has to carry heavy stuff, such as bags of food or logs of wood from the basement. It is very important for him to get some exercise. Thus, walking up the stairs has become part of his exercise program after the installation of the stair lift.

> I do not use the stair lift needlessly. I use it at autumn time and wintertime when going down for logs of wood or carrying several bags of food. I let the stuff stay in the first floor, walk upstairs to fetch the lift, and then sit down and go down again to fetch the bags. It is better to walk the stairs three times up and down daily, rather than cycling on an ergometer bike inside the apartment.

The lift inspires him to do exercises. It actually saves him energy that he can put towards other activities, such as maintaining or improving bodily functions or muscles.

> The lift inspires me to try to walk the stairs on my own in order to do physical exercises. At the same time, I use the lift when I really need it in order to save energy for other activities. Having the technologies (stair lift and car) even when you do not use them all the time is of great value. It also has to do with a feeling of safety.

The stair lift has several functions for Ted. First, it eases the burden for him and his wife on a daily basis. Second, Ted needs less informal help and has become less dependent on help from his wife. He did not have any formal help before the stair lift and does not need any afterwards. Third, easier access in and out of the building gives him and his family a greater feeling of safety. Fourth, the stair lift contributes to improving his physical health. It inspires him to do exercises, and it saves his energy for other activities. Doing exercises is important for him and does him good. As with Brian, the stairlift enables him to maintain an active social life. It also contributes to prolonging his independence from public services.

Less need for informal help

Richard is a 70-year-old married man with two adult children, one of whom lives at home. He lives with his wife, his daughter and his granddaughter on the second floor of a high house with eight floors. He has had a wheelchair lift (not a stair lift) for about 15 years. Before the installation, his family had to push him up and lift him down the stairs in front of the building. The wheelchair lift, however, is 'parked' in the basement and only goes to the first floor.

When he wants to get from the first floor to the second, he uses the ordinary lift. He has two electric outdoor wheelchairs, a rebuilt car, an electric adjustable bed, a flush toilet and an electric indoor rest chair. For Richard, using the lift that was installed some years ago in the building he lived in changed his life for the better: 'It has been perfect; I could not live without it. Yes, of course, I could have moved to a "handicap-house" or something or built something on my own. However, I am so terribly dependent upon this place'.

The lift saves him and his family lots of time and energy. Thus, an important asset of the stair lift is that it is a major help, not only to him, but also to his family. As with Ted, the lift reduces the amount of informal help needed. Nevertheless, Richard needs more help than Brian and Ted do. He needs help when he goes to the bathroom, when he has to change wheelchairs, when he takes a shower or when he needs to wash clothes. He also needs help to do the housework and with personal care. He receives a lot of informal aid, mainly from his wife, daughter and son. However, he drives his car on his own (it was rebuilt for him), and he uses the lift on his own. His favourite hobby is photography, and he spends a lot of time outside.

A change is about to come that will affect Richard's need for help with personal care. Taking a shower and using the toilet without assistance has become more difficult. An occupational therapist in the municipality took the initiative to help him rebuild the bathroom. One reason for this initiative is that his daughter is about to move out of the flat and cannot help him on a daily basis anymore. He gets no formal help from public services. With his daughter moving out, public health authorities plan to rebuild the bathroom as a new solution. The bathroom adaptation represents a kind of replacement of informal assistance, so that he can help himself when his wife is working, enabling him to stay in the flat alone without his daughter.

From a gender perspective, this points at an important issue. Rebuilding the bathroom as a result of his daughter's move can be seen as an example that adds to contemporary research on gender differences in care. Research has shown that in situations where parents have a daughter living at home or nearby, they are less inclined to receive help from public services (Berge, Øien and Jakobsson 2014). Both men and women assist their parents a lot, but this assistance is not equally distributed between the sexes. Daughters are the ones who typically give special effort to their parents (Berge et al. 2014). In our case, Ted is among the informants who needs the most assistance, but he gets no formal help. Maybe this is because he has a wife and a daughter helping him. Thus, the wheelchair elevator reduces informal help, not formal help, in this case.

Thea is an 85-year-old widow with three grown children. She lives alone in a block of flats with three floors. She has had a stair lift for about eight years. She manages her daily life more or less by herself, but she has weekly help from her children. She can cook for herself, and she does some housework. Her family helps her with washing and cleaning. Her daughter cleans the flat, her son does the shopping, and her daughter in law does the laundry. She uses the stair lift every day and walks outside using a rollator (wheeled walker). The stair lift has improved her quality of life very much. Walking up and down the stairs on her own is a great problem. She is not the only one in the building who uses the stair lift. She used to share the lift with a female neighbour downstairs. The two of them decided to apply for it at the same time, and they got it very fast. 'When Fred, the installer, came and said that the lift was ready, I said "Do I dare?"' She can still remember how it was to get it. 'I thought it was fantastic. Yes, 'Sit down', he said. We both tried it and found it wonderful'. She uses the stair lift every day and goes out for bingo, exercises and sometimes for a cup of coffee. 'That lift is the best thing that has happened to me. My quality of life has become much, much better. I cannot be without it. I did not know it existed'. It is evident that the stair lift is a great help for Thea. It enables her to be more social and more independent. Also in this case, the stair lift has had the greatest impact on the amount of informal care.

Retaining independence

Ann is a 72-year-old woman who lives alone in a big house with three floors. She has had a lift from the first floor to the second floor for about ten years. She also has a lift from the second floor to the third floor, for which she paid. She has two wheelchairs, one electric for outdoor use and one manual for indoor use. She is not able to pick up things from the floor, but uses special assistive devices. She needs assistance when getting into the stair lift and when changing wheelchairs. She gets some help from her brother who lives nearby. She also gets some help from two girlfriends who are her neighbours. Besides the informal help, she gets formal home help (housework) two days every second week. She also gets home nursing care once a week for washing her hair. 'I have help from the municipality once a week. It is good for me to be physically active. One has to make food and I like to have it tidy. The whole day goes. I have more than enough to do'.

She is very happy with the stair lifts. They have already enabled her to live in her own house for more than twelve years. Without the stair lifts, she would have had to move out. She loves her house and the garden that surrounds it. She says, 'Elderly people are fonder of their homes'. She says that it was her parents' house in the first place. Now she feels very much attached to it. She wants to manage everything by herself with as little help as possible, both formal and informally. She does not value or measure the stair lift in money. It is a matter of 'well-being and life and death', she says. She is happy to be able to stay on living in her own house, and she would never have been this happy in an institution for elderly people, she says.

Ann is entitled to more services and help from the municipality, but she resists more formal help. She wants to be active all day long. She cooks all her meals on her own and bakes bread. She is able to take a shower on her own but needs help to wash her hair. She can also get in bed and go to the toilet without assistance. She cannot go to the store to buy food anymore. However, by ordering food from a store that delivers to her house, she solved the problem. When she needs to go out by car, she uses the municipality transport services for wheelchair users. She is very fond of gardening. This means everything to her and makes her happy, she says. With the help of the stair lift and the wheelchair, she can get out. She can wheel around the house and do some gardening, such as planting vegetables.

The most important thing with the stair lifts in Ann's case is that they from the very beginning gave Ann the opportunity to retain her independence, to remain in her house for as long as possible and to age in place, with as little help as possible from family, neighbours or public services. Without the stair lifts, she would have had to move out of the house. Thus, to Ann the two stair lifts in her house are a matter of life and death. All that she wants is to live alone in the house that she loves, to be as active as possible and to manage most things on her own, irrespective of how long it takes.

Lisa is 82 years old and has had a stair lift installed in her house for the last four to five years. She lives with her husband in a semi-detached house with two floors. They have rebuilt their house so that she can stay at home as long as possible. She uses a powered wheelchair indoors and outdoors and has several other assistive technologies: electric chairs, an electric bed and a flush toilet. She needs help from others more or less all day long. All she can do is 'read, think, talk and use a computer', she says. She cannot eat without help. She gets home nursing care one hour twice a day for medicine and food (fed through a probe).

She cannot live in her house without the stair lift. She is very content with it. The stair lift makes her life a lot easier. It enables her to use the first floor and to get out of the house at any time, with the help of others. She has two personal assistants that assist her in her daily life, 40 hours per week. Her husband helps her a lot and does some of the housework. She also has one-hour home care every 14 days. It is obvious that the stair lift has qualitatively contributed to the enhancement of Lisa's life as it has enabled her to stay longer in her house with her husband, which is very important to them. In her case, the stair lift is of great help both to her husband (informal help) as well as to her personal assistants (formal help).

Trapped in the house – 'On the edge' to move to an institution

What follows now is based on interviews with two informants waiting for a stair lift to be installed in their homes. They are both eligible for such a lift, but they did not have it at the time of the interview. Their stories are very different from the others, focusing on (non-material) expenditures for both themselves and their families.

Karen is a 67-year-old married woman. She lives with her husband and her mother in a big house with three floors. Her husband participated during the interview. Her mother, whom she describes as very sporty, is 91 years old and lives on the top floor. Karen needs two lifts, one indoors between the first and second floors, and one outdoors from the garden to the street level.

Karen has problems moving around in the house. It is difficult for her to go out. She can hardly stand from a chair or the toilet, or walk around without assistance. She is able to walk alone down the stairs, but not up again. The toilets are downstairs. She has a chair in the shower to help her. She also has an alarm, due to falling. She is very dependent on her husband to help her stand up, walk and get into and out of the car. He is home on a long-term sick leave and helps her during the day. She also gets help from her mother, who cooks every day, and from a friend. She spends most of her day in her living room and rarely leaves her home.

In addition to informal help from family and friends, she gets home care and home nursing care once a week (washing and hair wash). She does not want a wheelchair. She thinks this will make her even more passive. Her husband is very sad because his wife is so dependent on him. It has become a burden to him, he says. He thinks his wife should live independently in her own house. They both think that it is *his* help and not the formal help that will be reduced by the stair lifts. The stair lifts will improve her quality of life a lot when installed.

It is obvious that in Karen's case the cost to the family of not having the stair lifts installed in the house is great. She is more or less trapped on one floor, unable to move around. She dreams of getting out to the garden. Her husband is home on a long-term sick leave, thus adding to the cost to the family (and society). He tries to help her as much as and as well as he can, but he is exhausted. Her 91-year-old mother does the cooking. Karen says that her mother is happy to do the cooking, but she and her husband also emphasise that something has to change to improve their quality of life and reduce the burden of helping Karen move around.

Hannah, who is 70 years old, is also waiting for a stair lift. She lives in a big house with two floors. She had just become a widow at the time of the interview (she lost her husband the week before). She lives on the upper floor. There, she has everything she needs. Downstairs is only a freezer and guest bedrooms. She looks forward to being able to use the first floor again, as for now it is very hard for her to walk down the stairs. She can walk a little bit. She goes out to fetch the newspaper every day, and she walks to the store. This, however, takes much longer than before – perhaps half an hour to buy a few groceries. She tries to avoid using the stairs as much as possible because of the time it takes. She has other technologies in the house: a shower chair, an electric working chair and a 'walking chair'. She is also waiting for a small lift to be installed that will enable her to use the bathtub.

She needs the stair lift to get to the first floor, to carry heavy bags of food and so on. She thinks her health will improve when she gets it. Now that her husband has died, she will receive more home care services, 70 minutes every second week. She also has a home care nurse every day for about 10 minutes or so; the nurse just pops in to see whether she is all right or if she needs anything. She can make food on her own, but she cannot do anything that requires physical exertion, like vacuum or wash the floors. It is likely that her husband's death will speed up the process of getting the staircase installed.

Conclusion

This chapter has presented the impact of stair lift installations on the quality of life for elderly people in order to help them age in place. Important issues include the positive effects of the stair lift on the user's independence, their participation in social life and their happiness to be able to stay longer in their own home. Stair lifts are housing adaptions that make houses or apartments more accessible. Without stair lifts, people cannot stay at home if they are too frail. In this chapter, we have seen that lifts have had a great impact on people's quality of life. The technology has many pros. In sum, it enables people to be more active outdoors, saves them energy that they can spend on physical exercises, reduces the need for informal care, allows independence and enables people to live longer at home.

An important finding is that the technology reduces informal care more than formal care. The family reaps the greatest advantage because they are the ones most likely to help. When the lift is installed, the user as well as his or her spouse saves energy, and many use the saved energy on other activities, such as physical exercise. Although it is impossible to generalize from this study, we have seen that daughters more than sons tend to provide informal help, and in one case, when the daughter moved out, new technology (initiated by the municipality) came in. It was only installed when she moved out, and not to relieve her when she lived at home.

In the long run, the staircase also reduces formal care and costs connected to formal care. The installation prolongs the time old people can live in their own homes, and we have shown that they are happy to age in place. It is thus efficient for society to install stair lifts when appropriate. Ultimately it reduces the amount of formal care spent on old people in institutions. The alternative is to move to an institution earlier than they wish, which is more costly for the society (Islam and Ravneberg 2012).

3 Disabled children's participation in sports and physical activities

Experiences and perceptions of assistive activity technologies

In western societies, the majority of children and young people participate in organised sports or physical activities at some point (Telama, Yang, Hirvensalo and Raitakari 2006; Strandbu and Øia 2007). In many countries, the number of participants in sport organisations has increased in recent decades (Telama et al. 2006). Participation in sports and physical activities has a positive impact on children's physical and psychological health, on their coping abilities and on their quality of life (King, Law, Hurley, Petrenchik and Schwellnus 2010). Furthermore, taking part in physical leisure activities during childhood is of significance for leading a physically active lifestyle in adulthood (Seippel, Abebe and Strandbu 2012). Thus, participation in physical activities is important for children and adults, and for non-disabled and disabled persons. Physical activity is important for our physical and psychological health and for our wellbeing and quality of life. Furthermore, and sometimes equally important, being a participant in sports or other physical activities represents a socially valued role that allows disabled persons to diminish the stigma of their physical disability (Taub, Blinde and Greer 1999). Compared to non-physical activities, sports and physical activities transpire in environments where competence and perceptions of disabled bodies may be altered.

Even though disabled children generally participate in leisure activities typical for their age group (Seim and Opsahl 2015), several studies indicate that they participate in leisure activities less frequently, especially sports and other physical leisure activities, than non-disabled children do (Majnemer et al. 2008; Ministry of Education 2008; Nyquist 2012). Furthermore, disabled children who do not participate in leisure activities are considered vulnerable, as they run a great risk of losing social support and becoming socially isolated (King et al. 2010; Bedell et al. 2013). Participation in sports can be a normalizing experience for disabled children that legitimates their social identity as 'typical' children (Taub and Greer 2000). Disabled children's participation in sports is found to enhance their peers' perceptions of their identity as social actors and to counter stigmatisation though demonstration of their athletic abilities (Taub et al. 1999). However, several factors influence disabled children's participation in sports and physical activities, including age, gender, activity limitations, family preferences, coping, motivation and environmental resources and supports (King et al. 2006; Shikako-Thomas, Majnemer, Law and Lach 2008). The literature also suggests that disabled children are less involved in sports and physical activities than their peers, and that their leisure activities are more passive and home-based and lack variety (Boström 2008; Imms, Reilly and Dodd 2008; Majnemer et al. 2008; Ministry of Education 2008; Shikako-Thomas et al. 2008; Engel-Yeger, Jarus, Anaby and Law 2009; King et al. 2010; Nyquist 2012).

Thus, the factors influencing disabled children's participation in sports and physical activities are complex and multifaceted. Nevertheless, in this chapter we will more closely examine disabled children's participation in sports and physical activities, and in particular their own experiences and perceptions of their use of assistive activity technologies. The chapter draws on a literature study of the subject, taking its point of departure from the literature of disability studies and childhood studies.

Childhood, participation and leisure time

Traditionally four different perspectives have characterised approaches to childhood studies: the psychological/developmental perspective, the educational/ behavioural perspective, the medical/individual perspective and the sociological/ socialisation perspective (Gulløv and Højlund 2003; Ytterhus, Egilson, Traustadòttir and Berg 2015). The sociological/socialisation perspective, also called childhood sociology (James, Jenks and Prout 2004), alters our perceptions of childhood. This perspective represents a break with the three other perspectives in that it gives children's own point of view and understanding a stronger voice than previous approaches have. Moreover, this perspective sees children as competent social actors with influence on their own lives. This means that children possess valuable expertise in actively and creatively designing their own identity, environment and society (James et al. 2004). Furthermore, children and childhood is not a fixed concept and does not have a fixed duration; rather, it is something that changes with time, place and history. This requires understanding childhood as a socially constructed entity. Consequently, it becomes important to investigate children's experiences in light of prevailing social and societal factors (James et al. 2004), such as participation in sports and physical activities.

Furthermore, children have the legal right to participate in all matters affecting them and as citizens in society (Gulbrandsen, Seim and Østensjø 2015). However, the term 'participation' has developed into a highly political and ideological notion, and its meaning is not always clear. Although children's participation can be investigated from an individual, personal perspective, as suggested by WHO's definition of participation as 'involvement in life situations' (ICF-CY 2007 p. 9), participation is also subject to social and cultural influences, especially participation related to social activities. While participation encompasses taking part in contextualised activities and social interactions in everyday life, it also includes the potential to make choices, have an influence and take risks. Strandbu (2011) divides participation into the following dimensions: (i) inclusion, that is, being a natural part of valuable settings; (ii) interaction, that is, doing or acting together; and (iii) meaning making, that is, having an impact and being acknowledged. We find that these dimensions of participation contain different, yet equally important elements of children's participation.

Leisure time activities may be investigated through four dimensions: *time* (how much), *activities* (what), *arena* (where) and *relations* (with whom) (Csikszentmihalyi 1997; Seim and Opsahl 2015). All these dimensions indicate preferences of affiliation and identity. In addition, leisure activities are categorised as formal or informal activities, or organised or non-organised activities. Non-organised activities are usually unplanned and initiated by children themselves. In contrast, organised activities are planned, structured and targeted activities that typically have a formal leader, trainer or instructor (King et al. 2004). Recent studies reveal that children participate in organised leisure activities more frequently today than in previous times (Seim and Opsahl 2015). In Norway, one of the most popular organisations providing leisure time activities for children is the Norwegian Confederation of Sports; one third of its members are children and young people (Strandbu and Øia 2007). However, we also know that the older children get, the less active they become, as nine-year-old children are more active than 15-year-old ones, and boys are more active than girls (Kolle, Steene-Johannessen, Klasson-heggebo, Andersen and Andersen 2009).

Disabled children, physical activity and assistive activity technologies

As adults, we need to remember that disabled children see themselves as ordinary children just like any other (Söderström and Ytterhus 2010; Asbjønslett, Helseth and Engelsrud 2014; Bekken 2014). Disabled children perceive their diagnosis or impairment as something they just happen to possess or manage; in their view, it is not a big deal (Söderström and Ytterhus 2010; Asbjørnslett, Helseth and Engelsrud 2014). Nevertheless, research has also shown that many physical disabled children, even those with only minor impairments, meet some additional challenges in everyday activities and in leisure activities (Østensjø 2005; Asbjørnslett 2015). Whether or not such challenges originate from individual, familiar, social or environmental factors may differ, just as the degree to which these challenges constitute barriers to participation may differ.

Disabled children, however, do participate in sports and physical activities in both organised and non-organised settings, and in both inclusive and segregated arrangements. The activities can range from informal play and sports to competitive sports on different athletic levels. However, it is difficult to estimate how many disabled children participate in sports and physical activities. Norwegian policy calls for 'open and inclusive sports', which is set as a goal for the Norwegian Confederation of Sports (Ingebrigtsen and Aspvik 2010), an overarching organisation for all sports organisations in Norway comprising 59 different sports federations and over 11,000 sports teams. Approximately 800–900 disabled Norwegian children are members of the Norwegian Confederation of Sports (Ingebrigtsen and Aspvik 2010). One of the sport federations oversees disabled children who participate in organised sports. The federation provides training and counselling for organising and adapting physical activities for disabled children. Their activities most often take place in local, segregated and adapted settings, are specifically targeted at disabled children, and are highly valued. Thus, although public policy and the sport federation's aim is open and inclusive sports activities, and although disabled children are included as members in ordinary local sports federations, most organised sports and physical activities for disabled children nevertheless take place in segregated settings.

Assistive technologies, and assistive activity technologies for use in leisure activities in particular, are not easily available in all countries. In some countries, however, including the Nordic countries, a wide range of assistive activity technologies is available to support disabled children's leisure activities. Assistive activity technologies are those assistive technologies that are specially designed to enable disabled people's participation in a variety of different physical activities, such as sports, outdoor activities and play. Such technologies include sit-skis, spike sleds, ski-walkers, arm-bicycles, tandem bikes and so forth. Disabled people who want to participate in sports or other physical activities can apply for the necessary assistive technology to perform that activity (Norwegian Labour and Welfare Administration 2014). When granted, the required assistive activity technologies are lent to the individual for as long as needed.

Studies show that the use of assistive activity technologies provides disabled children enhanced possibilities for mastering activities they would otherwise be unable to manage. Disabled children have emphasised that the possibilities these devices provided them to participate in activities with friends and family and to be independent in activities motivates them to use the devices frequently (Huang, Sugden and Beveridge 2009; Gjessing 2014). However, the types of devices used and the frequency with which children use them varies widely among children with the same type of physical difficulties, and research indicates that this variation is not due to the motor impairment in itself (Østensjø 2005). In this chapter, we explore disabled children's experiences and perceptions their use of assistive activity technologies, which enables us subsequently to discuss how we might explain the variation in disabled children's use of assistive activity technologies.

Disabled children's experiences with assistive activity technologies

In line with our understanding of children as competent social actors who possess valuable expertise, we will provide disabled children's own opinions and understandings a voice in this section. We do this by more closely examining the existing literature about disabled children's experiences with participation in physical leisure activities. Unfortunately, we have not been able to find a great deal of literature about children's personal views of the role of assistive activity technologies. However, in this chapter we draw on eight publications that highlight the voices of disabled children who participate in physical leisure activities, with two publications that focus on the role of assistive activity technologies. Even though the disabled children's experiences of assistive activity technologies are multifaceted, interrelated and variable, we have chosen to present them here in a more disjointed way in the service of making them more transparent.

Experiences of the devices' properties

Most disabled children are quite familiar with AT, since many of them have used AT from early childhood and have experienced changes in equipment as they grow and develop. Huang et al. (2009) found that because of this long-term experience, disabled children generally regard AT as helpful. They cite one child who talked about his ankle-foot-orthotics (AFO) in this way: 'My walking posture looks better . . . and I can perform activities better, . . . so I feel they are quite helpful for me' (Huang et al. 2009:99). In this same study, several disabled children stated that their opportunities for participation and interaction improved through use of AT; as one ten-year-old boy put it: 'I can play with other children with the help of the devices. Without the devices I can't play with them or join in a game with them. Maybe I will then lose some friends' (Huang et al. 2009:100).

Because disabled children have used AT for most of their lives, it can be difficult for them to remember how they acquired it. In Gjessing's study (2014) a boy who has outgrown his tricycle and switched to a new one, says about the change:

> I got it free. We just asked the woman. . . . I don't remember her name, but she told us to come where there are many bicycles, and when we arrived there and looked for a bike we picked this one.
>
> (p. 29)

Other children in the study described AT as arriving 'in the mail or something' and said that they tried it out together with their parents.

The ability to participate in activities with other children, rather than just watching them, is the most common reason disabled children provide for their need of assistive activity technologies. Typical words they use to describe what it would be like not to have the assistive activity technologies are 'stupid' and 'boring' (Gjessing 2014). Most disabled children are aware that their equipment for physical activities is different from their peers' equipment. Even so, some nevertheless describe the sort of tricycle they use as an 'ordinary' bicycle. Others think their assistive activity devices are 'nice' and 'practical'.

When it comes to AT for children, designers have more freedom to emphasize than they do for adult AT devices. Thus, AT devices for children are usually more stylish and colourful than adult AT devices. One AT designer explains why this is the case: 'Children have this tendency to wear out their AT, and their AT is more age specific than AT for adults. Consequently, there is no focus on reuse of children's devices, such as it is when it comes to AT for adults.' The focus on reuse of AT for adults is rooted in economic issues and is therefore a vital factor in the public allocation system.

Many disabled children are aware that using assistive activity technology may connote disability and that the visible nature of their devices can easily attract unwanted attention. Even so, most disabled children express acceptance of these technologies because of the benefits they provide, and they attach a positive value to the technologies (Huang et al. 2009). We understand this as a result of their experiences with the assistive activity devices that enable them to participate, interact and perform activities with friends and peers.

Experiences of physical activities

The possibility of experiencing activities that involve speed, possible risks and certainly excitement are factors that motivate many disabled children to try out assistive activity technologies. Gjessing (2014) found that many disabled children think it is more exciting to use a tricycle or tandem bike than a wheelchair because they can vary the pace more on a bike and because they can experience speed and excitement on more equal terms with friends. In response to a question about what he thinks about biking, one boy said, 'When you . . . well especially downhill . . . I think it is fun to have speed when I bike with friends' (Gjessing 2014:32). Another thing children appreciate is the extended range of motion a bike provides.

Trying out new things for the first time is not always easy and takes some courage. As a result, seeing other disabled children and young people 'in action' performing activities and managing assistive technologies is often an inspiration and trigger for disabled children to try out new activities and new technologies. This is very often the way disabled children are introduced to new activities. As one boy told Gjessing (2014:33) about the first time he observed another disabled young person skiing on an alpine hill, 'It looked a lot of fun and I wanted to try it out too.' Another boy described downhill skiing as 'a lot of fun' and explained the pleasurable sense of speed it provides:

> I am sure we reached 50 kilometres per hour. It is just foommm, fooom, fooom, and then we are down the hill. It is as if you feel more alive when you ski and it's a little bit crazy so to speak than when you sit in a wheelchair.
>
> (p. 33)

In addition to the fun and excitement it provides, many children say that they are motivated to use assistive activity technologies because these technologies enable them to play with their peers and join them in shared activities. One 11-year-old girl explained it thus: 'I can play with my classmates; I can do many things with them together' (Huang et al. 2009:101). A boy who uses his spike toboggan with friends on the ice court, where sometimes the toboggan becomes a joint activity device, says, 'Ehh, well sometimes people stand behind[,] skating and pushing my toboggan, and then we run very fast' (Gjessing 2014:34).

However, not all experiences are entirely positive. Children also recount that they sometimes become tired and discouraged when using assistive activity technologies. This is often due to physical exhaustion, lagging behind their peers or being dependent on help. Moreover, as children grow older, it is even harder for them to keep up with non-disabled peers. This may cause them to quit the activity or to seek other activities specifically adapted for disabled children. Nyquist (2012) spoke with an 11-year-old boy who uses a wheelchair and asked him what he enjoys doing in his leisure time. He answered:

> I enjoy playing soccer the most. It is what all my friends do. My teacher makes sure that I get to play, even though I'm not playing for real. However, I have won an el-bandy match for real. El-bandy is fun to play. My brother plays it too, and Iver. Iver is my friend. He plays too, even though he does not have a wheelchair. He can borrow one, but that chair is not as nice as mine is. I have my own el-bandy wheelchair that I use only for el-bandy.
>
> (p. 273)

While we know that disabled children generally participate in sports and physical activities less frequently than their non-disabled peers (King, Law, King, Rosenbaum, Kertoy and Young 2003; Shikako-Thomas et al. 2008; King et al. 2010), studies have also revealed that sport adaptation increases disabled children's participation in sports and physical activities (Kalyvas and Reid 2013). However, whether or not the activities are adapted, the factor that most motivates disabled children to participate is enjoyment and interactions with friends and peers (Majnemer et al. 2008; Huang et al. 2009; Nyquist 2012; Gjessing 2014).

Furthermore, it has also been revealed that disabled children themselves seldom take the initiative to engage in physical activities. Usually, their parents take the initiative to have them engage in informal physical activities. Sometimes parents even reward their children for using an assistive activity technology, especially if the child does not want to use it or is wary of it (Gjessing 2014). As one girl explained to Gjessing (2014), 'I am a little sceptical doing this, but if I do it, I get a reward from Dad' (p. 36). Another girl put it this way: 'It's mostly Mom or Dad who suggests that we go hiking or biking. Then I have to use my AT. Usually I don't make the suggestion' (p. 36). When questioned why she didn't suggest the activity, she answered, 'It's not a big deal for me'. A boy recounted that, when he wants to go out in his powered wheelchair, his mother often suggests he take his tricycle instead, and then he does just that (Gjessing 2014).

Many disabled children engage in physical activities together with their families, some simply for the company, and some because they need assistance. Especially for winter activities, disabled children depend on company to assist them. One boy told Gjessing (2014) that he did not engage with friends in winter activities as often. When he cross-country skied, he did it with his father 'because I go a little faster when Dad drags me'. Sometimes he went skiing with his mother, 'but then it goes a little slower' (p. 40). Huang et al. (2009) found that when the social climate encouraged independence and facilitated interaction with peers and friends, disabled children showed a great eagerness to achieve independence with the help of their assistive devices. Experiences of being able to execute tasks that they otherwise are unable to do lead to disabled children attaching a constructive meaning to their assistive devices and describing them as opening a whole new world to them (Huang et al. 2009). This new world may be participation in exciting activities in new places and new settings, but just as much may mean being a natural part of a valued group in a valued setting.

Experiences of the significance of participation in physical leisure activities

Four factors in particular reoccur when disabled children speak about why they participate in physical leisure activities. These factors are (i) that the activities are fun, (ii) that the assistive devices are cool, (iii) that they can participate with friends and family and (iv) that they can participate in normal and common activities (Huang et al. 2009; Nyquist 2012; Gjessing 2014; Asbjørnslett 2015). The disabled children Huang et al. (2009) spoke with said that use of their devices not only provided great fun but also made them enjoy the friendship of their peers and gave them a sense of belonging to a group. A similar sentiment was also the essence of what children told Gjessing (2014): that they appreciated the opportunities the assistive activity technologies provided them to be together with friends, doing the same things their friends did and at the same pace they did them. The children whom Asbjørnslett, Helseth and Engelsrud (2014) interviewed echoed the children in Gjessing's study when they emphasised the significant cultural value of participation in sports-related activities. One boy whom Asbjørnslett et al. (2014) spoke with put it this way: 'Playing and talking about football is normal' (p. 327). On the other hand, another boy said, 'I think it's a little dumb that so many students are so interested in football. They want to play it a lot, and I find it difficult' (p. 328). Another boy who had a progressive disease changed his role on the local handball team from that of an active player to playing with 'different rules' and subsequently to cheering the team along from the sidelines. Asbjørnslett et al. (2014) found that even though participation in physical activities created challenges for many disabled children, it also provided them opportunities for fun, enjoyment, learning and social participation.

The frequency with which disabled children participate in physical activities with friends varies. In Gjessing's (2014) study, disabled children participated in organised leisure activities one or two nights per week. These activities included swimming, football, table tennis, horseback riding or floor ball. The most common reasons the children provided for participating in these activities were 'because then you get to be a part of a team and get to know other people' and 'I have a lot of cool friends there' (p. 41). Nyquist (2012) found that disabled children want to participate in physical leisure activities and that they tend to do so in their local community with friends and family members. Nyquist refers to an interview with an 11-year-old boy who enjoyed playing football. He said that he enjoyed football because that was what all his friends did. He continued, 'I used to be a football referee, but not anymore. My friends got a little annoyed if I did anything wrong . . . but I can't roll fast enough, at least not on the grass'. Nyquist found that several disabled children viewed team sports in particular as important and fun, even though they had quit the team or did not participate in matches and tournaments. However, the children did not seem to care too much about this; rather, it was a pure statement instead of a subject described in detail. The interviews quickly turned to what they did instead. The ability to be an active member of a group and to promote their own solutions for implementing their participation is of great significance for disabled children's participation in physical leisure activities. However, their participation is also characterised by unpredictability and varying accessibility. Small nuances in adaptations and reactions from friends and teammates appear significant to disabled children's opportunities for participation in physical leisure activities. Such nuances may be crucial to whether the child experiences acknowledgement as a natural part of the team and has an impact on the setting.

Discussion

In the process of working with or studying disabled children and their everyday lives, it is vital to understand how disability, society and technology are experienced, constructed and influenced by institutions, adults and peers, as well as by the disabled children themselves. We know that social acceptance and peer intimacy depend on opportunities for social participation with peers in leisure activities (Wendelborg and Kvello 2010). Moreover, environmental, family and child characteristics also affect social participation (Imms 2008; Majnemer et al. 2008; Huang et al. 2009). Taking this into consideration, in our context we strive to give the children a prominent voice. This means giving attention to how they view their participation in different leisure activities and environments and seeking their opinions about helpful supports. Gjessing (2014) found that children experienced a short travel distance to activities and accessible activity arenas as helpful supports for using their assistive activity devices and for participation in physical leisure activities. Furthermore, the children highlighted the importance of being able to use the devices independently and the positive attitudes of family, friends and coaches. These things facilitated their motivation to participate and provided the children experiences of having fun, having an impact and being acknowledged. In addition, we believe that it is important to bear in mind that opportunities to engage in physical activities provide disabled children more than the joy and excitement of the moment, as mastery of experiences in one activity creates confidence that is likely transferable to other activities, arenas and settings.

Disabled children are willing to make great efforts based on their own perceptions of their peers' leisure time behaviour. These children usually develop strategies to overcome limitations and will constantly adapt to their life situation as active social agents. (Asbjørnslett et al. 2014). It is common among children and young people to want to be able to choose their leisure activities themselves and to choose between ordinary inclusive activities and special adapted activities. Although this might seem obvious, it turns out that this is not always the case for disabled Norwegian children. Leisure activity options vary a great deal between local municipalities. In some local municipalities, there are many options, and in other municipalities, they are more limited (Ministry of Education 2008).

Although research on disabled children's use of assistive activity technologies in physical leisure activities is scarce, the available research leaves little doubt that disabled children's use of such devices does promote their participation in physical leisure activities otherwise inaccessible to them (Huang et al. 2009; Gjessing 2014). However, exploring the ways in which this technology might promote their participation in such activities requires knowledge of the individual child's preferences and of the range of technological possibilities.

As there is an extremely diverse range of assistive activity devices, it might be challenging to provide an overview of all the possibilities. Thus, it might be appropriate to contact a technology competence centre, a supplier or other AT professionals. In this way parents, teachers, therapists or others who want to apply for assistive activity devices might receive some advice about relevant devices for the specific activity and child. The explosion of technological development has had both positive and negative consequences in terms of disabled children's possibilities for participation. On the positive side, the expansion of technology has increased the accommodation options. On the negative side, it has made it difficult to identify the best technology for a specific activity for a particular child. Consequently, the process of matching children and technology has become more complex, and expectations and preferences vary widely. Gamble, Dowler and Orslene (2006) describe a model for appropriate AT selection for vocational outcomes. We find the key points in their model applicable for appropriate AT selection for disabled children's physical leisure activities as well. These key points are as follows: (i) explore the child's activity readiness and preferences, (ii) identify relevant activities, (iii) identify available resources in the local community, (iv) explore and adapt appropriate AT, (v) assess AT and child in the relevant activity and (vi) assess AT and child in the activity in a natural setting. Applying these key points is vital in choosing the right activity device for a particular child. Additionally, it is important to bear in mind that children usually benefit from testing the devices in environments they find familiar and safe. Having the necessary knowledge of AT and skills while working through a systematic selection process is critical to successful outcomes in AT allocation. Moreover, it is highly recommended to include the AT user, in our case the disabled child, in all phases of the AT selection (Gamble et al. 2006).

Concluding remarks

The characteristics of accessible and inclusive sports and physical activities are complex and diverse and may vary depending on who participates. Nevertheless, what disabled children themselves find characteristic of good, accessible and inclusive physical leisure activities can be summarised as *possibilities to choose*. This means, among other things, the possibility to choose between ordinary but inclusive organised physical activities and specially adapted organised physical activities. Disabled children are as diverse and individual as any other children are, and some of them might prefer one setting, while others prefer another. However, disabled children generally want their activities to be accessible, to be group based yet adaptable, and to facilitate social relationships with friends and peers (Huang et al. 2009; Gjessing 2014). This last characteristic becomes more and more important the older children get and is especially prominent in the transition from childhood to youth. In this phase, the desire for liberation from parents grows, a desire that is challenging for disabled children, as they are usually more dependent on their parents and dependent for a longer period than most other children and young people. Accessible arenas for inclusive activities and social relationships outside the family and home are therefore even more important for disabled children and young people.

Moreover, disabled children's use of assistive activity technologies is affected by their perception of different aspects of the devices, the environment and the benefits the devices provide. In this respect, it is important to remember that children's views often differ from those of adults. Thus, a greater effort is needed to include disabled children's voices in general research about their participation in sports and physical activities, and particularly in research about their experiences and perceptions of assistive activity technologies.

4   Inclusive education and the effects of assistive technologies

After years of separate education systems for students with special needs, today's prevailing view is that such educational segregation should be avoided and that all children should be educated with their peers in mainstream schools. Inclusive schools are perceived as 'the most effective means of combating discriminatory attitudes, creating welcoming communities, building an inclusive society and achieving education for all; moreover, they provide an effective education to the majority of children and improve the efficiency and ultimately the cost-effectiveness of the entire educational system' (UNESCO 1994:9). This perspective goes beyond valuing the inclusion of all in a common education system; it also sees an inclusive education system as a means to develop a society that welcomes diversity. Several countries have committed to this perspective by signing declarations and conventions that state the intention of providing every student with an acceptable level of education, regardless of the student's individual characteristics, abilities, interests and learning needs (UNESCO 1994). The goal of such an inclusive education policy is to enable full participation for all students in environments and activities that are commonly shared and positively valued and to remove arrangements that are devalued and stigmatised, such as special arrangements for disabled students (Tøssebro and Lundeby 2002).

Against this background, the subject of this chapter is everyday school life and use of AT by disabled students in mainstream schools. The chapter investigates how use, or non-use, of AT in everyday school life influences disabled students' opportunities to actively participate in ordinary classroom activities. This investigation draws on two ethnographic studies of disabled students' everyday school life that were conducted in Norwegian primary and secondary mainstream schools.

Although the number of disabled students in mainstream schools has increased through the practice of 'inclusive' education, this does not mean that disabled students are fully included in all aspects of school life. Research shows a progression away from mainstream classroom participation towards special education practices outside the regular classroom as students with special needs grow older (Wendelborg and Tøssebro 2010; Wendelborg 2014). This decreased classroom participation takes place more and more from the age of 10. Moreover, this decrease is more significant for children whose disabilities are categorised as moderate or severe, as opposed to students with mild or solely physical disabilities. However, this decrease is not necessarily caused by the student's impairment. Rather, it tends to be caused by the relation between the individual student's characteristics and the demands of the environment; the gap between students with learning difficulties or complex disabilities and their peers becomes more evident as they grow older (Wendelborg and Tøssebro 2010). As students age, school activities require more intellectual abilities, and the discrepancy between learning outcomes and individual students' capacities becomes more telling. This discrepancy makes it even more challenging for teachers to provide satisfactory learning adapted to individual students. To address such a challenge, responsibility for students with special needs is frequently delegated to special educators or school assistants. This may indicate that the class teacher is expected to have responsibility for 'ordinary students', while special educators and assistants are responsible for 'special students' (Wendelborg and Tøssebro 2010).

Barriers to an inclusive education, such as the differentiation between students described above, are attributed to the persistence of a medical model of understanding disability as an individual phenomenon (Wendelborg and Tøssebro 2010; Lalvani 2013). The medical model of understanding disability assumes that disabilities are caused by individual characteristics or deviances. Such an understanding has implications for how special needs are understood and how education for students with special needs is shaped (Froestad and Ravneberg 2006). An individual approach to students with special needs reflects such an understanding, and those who adopt such an understanding often believe that the most effective way to teach special needs students is to provide intensive educational support outside the regular classroom (Wendelborg and Tøssebro 2010; Lalvani 2013). Such a medical, individual understanding of disability is reflected in many school organisations through an emphasis on the individual student's diagnosis, shortcomings or deficits as a prerequisite for administrative allocation of money or human resources, such as a special educator. In this way, administrative practice maintains the traditional distinction between 'ordinary' and 'special' students (Markussen, Strømstad, Carlsten, Hausstätter and Nordahl 2007; Kermit, Tharaldsteen, Haugen and Wendelborg 2014).

Research suggests that disabled students in mainstream schools participate less frequently in school activities than their non-disabled classmates do, and they have less access to curriculum activities than their non-disabled classmates (Shevlin, Kenny and McNeela 2002; Erikson, Welander and Granlund 2007). Being included comprises more than being present. Being included in a mainstream school means 'being in an ordinary school with other students, learning the same curriculum, at the same time, in the same classroom, with full acceptance by all in a way which makes the student feels no different from any other student' (Bailey 1998:184). This means that inclusion is achieved only when the concept of inclusion has really lost its content and no distinction remains between 'ordinary' and 'special' students.

An inclusive school context

In Norway, a decentralisation of power from central school authorities to those on the local level has taken place over the last decade. This new delegation of power to local school authorities means that students' educations largely depend on local priorities and variations in available resources. This shift has led to a concern that the spotlight on the ideology of inclusive education is at risk of being lost (Wendelborg 2014). This concern is also applicable to several other countries, including the United Kingdom (Riddle 2007; Byrne 2013) and the United States (Lalvani 2013). The Norwegian public ideology holds that when special education is needed, this education shall take place in a regular classroom setting together with classroom peers. Nevertheless, there has been a documented development of establishing more and more special classes within regular mainstream schools and of using a variety of segregated arrangements for disabled students (Tøssebro, Engan and Ytterhus 2006; Wendelborg 2010). Even when disabled students attend local mainstream schools and are members of regular classes, they may not be included in the ordinary classroom setting. Furthermore, how the individual local school is organised has proven to be of vital importance for disabled students' possibilities to participate and be included (Wendelborg 2010; Wendelborg and Kvello 2010; Wendelborg and Tøssebro 2010). This means that despite the effort to promote an inclusive school system, exclusion and marginalisation of disabled students still occurs within Norwegian mainstream schools. Viewed against this background, the question is how disabled students' use of AT promotes or inhibits their participation in regular classroom activities in mainstream schools.

We have found indications that the implementation and appropriate use of AT in ordinary classroom settings may reverse the trend of increased segregation as students grow older. Research shows that this occurs when school staff members have positive attitudes towards AT, the AT is high quality and the AT is frequently and easily used (Rekkedal 2012; Rekkedal 2013; Øien, Fallang and Østensjø 2015). Use of AT also reverses the trend of increased segregation when the students experience immediate benefits from AT use, such as enhanced selfhood, social participation, skills and learning (Craddock 2006; Hemmingsson, Lindström and Nygård 2009; Huang et al. 2009; Murchland and Parkyn 2010). Thus, deliberate and targeted AT use in ordinary classroom settings may serve as a powerful tool to promote inclusive education.

Socio-material practices

AT use by disabled students in classroom activities is found to support inclusive education (Craddock 2006; Hemmingsson et al. 2009; Huang et al. 2009). However, AT use is not only an individual modification; it also depends on a variety of compatible connections and relationships, including human, technological and organisational entities (Moser 2003; Söderström 2012). Moreover, several studies have determined that AT assigned for use in school is sometimes used as intended, but quite often is used less frequently than intended, is used in unintended ways, or is totally abandoned altogether (Murchland and Parkyn 2010; Söderström 2012). These incorrect uses may be due to technical barriers, but are most often due to human barriers connected to lack of competence or insecurity and attitudes (Lindsay 2010; Rekkedal 2013; Smith 2013). The purpose of this chapter is to highlight some of the unintentional consequences of everyday socio-material practices that take place in the classroom.

Socio-material practices are everyday actions and interactions carried out through use of various human and non-human resources, such as our bodies, analogue instruments and/or digital tools. A socio-material practice implies that the different resources put to use, whether human or non-human, are all actors connected in a network that mutually reinforce each other (Moser 2006; Latour 2008). Socio-material practices may include the use of AT in classrooms; the question then becomes how AT use influences a disabled pupil's opportunities for participation, and how these opportunities affect the pupil. In other words, how is a disabled pupil's participation made and unmade in specific interactions containing both human and material elements?

ANT

Participation

In the inclusive education debate, social participation is seen as a key issue (Bossaert, Colpin, Pijl and Petry 2013). However, the meaning of 'social participation' is not always clear, and it needs to be distinguished from other, related concepts in order to provide guidelines for the current inquiry. The concept of participation has been defined in a variety of ways. One definition of this concept widespread both in research and in professional practice comes from WHO. In *International Classification of Functioning, Disability and Health: Children and Youth Version* (ICF-CY), WHO defines participation as 'involvement in a life situation' (WHO 2007:9). In this definition, involvement encompasses taking part, being accepted, belonging, being included or being engaged in an area of life or having access to needed resources (WHO 2007). However, this definition has been criticised for being vague and for excluding the subjective dimension and subjective experiences. Coster and Khetani (2008) point out that when researching participation, it is important to distinguish activity from participation and to distinguish objective dimensions of participation from subjective ones. Witsø (2013) distinguishes among participation's emotional, practical and intellectual dimensions.

In this chapter, social participation is conceptualised as social *interaction*, in line with Bossaert et al. (2013), who state that social interaction is generally perceived as verbal or non-verbal communicative behaviours towards a classmate or adult. Such social interaction may be observed as students spend free time together, complete tasks together or do group activities. A lack of or limited interactions are thus an indicator of social isolation (Bossaert et al. 2013). Depending on the subject of investigation, students' participation can be studied in different ways: talking with students about their experiences (emotional participation), observing interactions (practical participation) or including students in the research (intellectual participation). In inclusive education, more knowledge about the importance of ongoing intended and unintended interaction processes during class, that is, the significance of practical participation, is needed. This chapter devotes attention to participation as practical *socio-material interactions* observed during an ordinary school day in regular classrooms in mainstream schools.

Everyday school life and the effects of assistive technologies

Classrooms are composed of people, relationships, tools and technologies that all operate as mediating devices. Through this mediation, meanings are negotiated until a shared understanding is reached via the flow of socio-material practices in the classroom. In this section, the flows of these practices are investigated, shedding light on how contextual dynamic connections among environments, locations, technologies, and humans influence disabled pupils' participation.

Location in the classroom

A disabled student's location in the classroom is important for his or her opportunities to interact with classmates and participate in classroom activities (Murchland and Parkyn 2010). The need to give special attention to location varies depending on the individual student's need for accommodation. While hard-of-hearing students need certain kinds of accommodations, visually impaired students need other kinds of accommodations, just as students with learning difficulties and students with mobility difficulties need yet other kinds of accommodations. However, they all require some special consideration as to their location within the classroom in order to make use of their potential. The significance of location is illustrated here with a glimpse of Joachim's everyday school life. Joachim is a 13-year-old boy who uses a powered wheelchair to get around.

> Joachim is seated in his wheelchair in the back of the classroom alongside three other boys. The teacher gives the class some instructions for group work and how the pupils should work during the lesson. Joachim turns in his wheelchair towards the other boys in the back row, and they put their heads together. They talk together while they browse some books and take notes.

The boys in the back row collaborate on the group work assignment through talking, reading, and taking notes. This group collaboration requires proximity between its participants. The setting highlights connections among humans (the pupils), objects (books, desks, etc.) and technologies (wheelchair, computer); these connections constitute a socio-material practice that is contextual (group work assignment), dynamic (task solving) and relational (collaboration). In this context, Joachim's location within the classroom facilitates his participation in classroom activities and allows him to demonstrate his abilities as a competent classmate.

However, Joachim and his classmates are not always located in their regular classroom; quite often they move to other teaching areas, which is a common occurrence for most classes. In the next excerpt, Joachim's class is taking place in a small auditorium. In this auditorium, Joachim is located in his wheelchair on the floor in front of and below the auditorium's rows of chairs.

> The teacher is standing, talking and moving around. Most of the time, she stands close to the first row of seats; then she is actually standing behind

Joachim. Consequently, Joachim is sitting alone in his wheelchair in the front, with all his classmates and the teacher behind him. After some instructions the pupils begin their assignment, and it becomes quiet in the auditorium. After some time, Joachim stops writing. At this point many of his classmates have begun to whisper together, some about their assignment and some about other things; only a few continue to write. Joachim sits alone, does nothing and stares at the wall.

This excerpt illuminates how disabled students' opportunities to participate and interact emerge as contextual, dynamic connections among environments, locations, technologies and humans. Østensjø, Carlberg and Vøllestad (2005) point to the importance of environmental modifications in promoting disabled students' social functioning. Environmental modifications can include AT, but also may include any kind of fixed or removable adaptations and locations used to maximise a student's performance in everyday activities. When an environmental area changes, the need for modifications change, and if this change is not accounted for, opportunities for participation also change, often for the worse. Students who depend on large or different types of AT are especially vulnerable to changes to environmental areas, such as changes in classrooms.

Implementation of technology

It is a challenge for many teachers to employ teaching strategies that continuously support special needs students' participation in the dynamic of socio-material classroom practices. This is especially evident when locations or activities change. The significance of a teacher's constant awareness and purposeful AT use is illustrated here by a look into the everyday school life of Eva, an 11-year-old girl who is hard of hearing:

Eva sits in the middle of the desk column by the window. She is wearing hearing aids and a body-worn FM receiver; the teacher is wearing a microphone headset, and all pupils have handheld microphones. The teacher starts teaching the class at the blackboard. When pupils answer the teacher's questions, most of the time they do not use their microphones. Sometimes the teacher reminds them to do so, and sometimes she doesn't. After a while, the pupils start working individually, and the teacher walks around to help. At this point the teacher has turned off her microphone. Some of the pupils start talking together. Sometimes a pupil asks a question out loud, and the teacher answers out loud, but now none of them use their microphones. Eva is working on her assignment, but she spends more time looking around in the classroom at pupils talking to each other than at her assignment.

The teacher's and students' constant shifts between use and non-use of the microphones exclude Eva from vital parts of teaching, such as clarifying details and specific examples. In addition, the students' failure to use microphones for small talk deprives Eva of the possibility to participate in their social chatter. In this context, Eva is constantly pushed into and out of the flow of classroom conversation based on whether the teacher and students use their microphones.

The teacher seems to be aware of the significance of microphone use when she teaches the class as a whole, but she seems to forget the significance of this technology during spontaneous dialogue between her and other students. Answering questions about microphone use, she replies, 'I try to use it the whole time, but I easily forget when I am not at the blackboard'. This reveals an awareness of including Eva in joint teaching but also a lack of recognition of the significance of Eva's inclusion in spontaneous talk, whispering and discrete interactions during a lesson. This can be interpreted as an underlying misperception of disability as an individual phenomenon, requiring teaching strategies directed at individual students and not when addressing others. Such an interpretation corresponds with research that attributes barriers to classroom participation to the persistence of a medical understanding of disability (Boer, Pijl and Minnaert 2011; Lalvani 2013; Shevlin, Winter and Flynn 2013).

While teachers sometimes express positive attitudes towards inclusion and AT use, it sometimes turns out that teachers find AT use too troublesome. Anders is an 11-year-old boy who has been allocated a Memo Planner, a colourful digital board designed to hang on the wall. It is designed to help Anders gain an overview of all school activities by visually displaying different activities, including what time and where they take place. Anders' teacher explains, 'We don't use the Memo Planner because Anders gets so preoccupied by the Planner's lights, colours, and buttons, and there is no time to spend getting to know new technologies'. To gain familiarity with AT and learn how to utilise its potential takes time, and time is scarce for most teachers.

Even though AT implementation may be initially time-consuming, AT use in the classroom has been found to be dependent on teachers' willingness to integrate it into their teaching strategies. The more positive a teacher is towards technology overall, the more likely he or she is to integrate AT in the classroom (Rekkedal 2013). Several studies have found that AT assigned for use in schools is frequently abandoned (Murchland and Parkyn 2010; Söderström 2012). This may be the result of frustration with AT for not working as expected (Pape et al. 2002; Söderström and Ytterhus 2010) or of a teacher's lack of time, interest or knowledge when it comes to technology (Söderström 2012).

When AT works as expected and is implemented in ordinary classroom settings, disabled students find it very intriguing. When asked what they think of AT, they say such things as 'I think AT is an ingenious invention', 'I would be lost without it' and 'It would be a boring life without it'. The following scene from a fifth grade maths class illustrates the significance of implementing assistive AT in ordinary classroom settings.

Lisa has severe movement difficulties and sits in a powered wheelchair at a large desk. The teacher asks the class to solve the maths problems on specific pages in the math book. An assistant helps Lisa start the maths program on her computer, and Lisa uses a joystick to navigate the marker on the screen to solve the same maths tasks as the rest of the class. One by one, the maths problems appear on the screen, proposing several possible answers. Lisa uses the joystick to click on the answer she thinks is correct. She is given points when she clicks on the right answer – more points for more difficult maths tasks – and when clicking on the wrong answer, she is given no points. Lisa navigates the marker around the screen using the joystick. It is sometimes a little bit hard for her to stop the marker exactly at the correct answer because she has some involuntary movements in her upper limbs. However, most of the time she stops the marker at the correct answer, and at the end of maths class she has many points. Lisa proudly shows her points to her classmates, who stop at her desk and compliment her before storming out to recess.

In this maths class, the socio-material practice of implementing AT in the ordinary classroom setting enabled Lisa to participate and demonstrate her competence in 'being ordinary' (Goffman 1963), and thus pass as an ordinary student in maths class. Lisa's participation in the ordinary maths class is here enabled through three interrelating circumstances: (i) her mastery of useful technologies, (ii) her presence and participation in classroom activities, and (iii) her classmates' recognition of her competence – all vital elements of socio-material practices.

This investigation of what is done in practice, what it emerges from, and what effects it creates reveals how socio-material practices are not predetermined, but are effects of socio-material interactions, relations and orderings. For assistive ICT to promote disabled students' enhanced participation in ordinary classroom activities, these technologies must work satisfactorily, which requires commitment from several sources as well as close interdisciplinary collaboration.

Interdisciplinary collaboration

Ensuring disabled students enjoy the benefits of using AT requires concerted effort from many different actors. Regular testing, customisation, training, operation and maintenance of equipment are prerequisites for appropriate use of the equipment. Actors involved in this work include occupational therapists, AT centres, various centres of expertise, technical suppliers, teachers, the local school's information technology manager and the municipality. Coordinating the combined efforts of all these actors is a challenge, and the responsibility for coordinating this collaboration is usually very unclear. How many teachers experience this confusion is described by one of Anna's teachers:

> The hardest part is actually finding out who is responsible for what when it comes to maintenance, upgrading and training in using the equipment. That is, how responsibility is formally divided between the school, the assistive technology centre and the resource centre.

Before this teacher began working with Anna, he received no training or guidance in how to use her AT. However, he is a young and dedicated teacher and is not afraid to try new things, so he has taught himself how to use most of Anna's AT. Initially, he felt a little overwhelmed because it was so much equipment to master at once. To be able to do his job, he believes it is imperative that he is unafraid to try new things and that he is interested in technology. Both the AT centre and resource centre offer various courses on the AT equipment that Anna uses. However, the teacher had not received any information about these courses, and he was unaware that such a service existed. It is usually not the lack of relevant courses that is the problem but rather that teachers lack the opportunity to attend them for various reasons (Bekken 2009).

The AT centre organises several courses on the use of various assistive ICT. The courses are free, and the AT centre provides information about their courses to the local municipality's contact person for AT. This means that information about the courses has to go through several channels before reaching its target. In the case of teachers in mainstream schools, for example, this information goes from the AT centre to the local contact person, then to the management at the local school and finally to the teacher in question. The information very often gets lost somewhere along this path. Moreover, in cases where this information actually reaches the local school, it is entirely up to the school if they want to use the offered courses. Even though the courses are free, attending these courses is nevertheless an economic issue. If a teacher attends a course for one day, the school has to hire a substitute, which entails an expense. When resources are scarce, schools have to prioritise, and courses and professional development are usually not priorities. Courses and teacher education, however, are not always a prerequisite for ensuring all students participate. Anna's mother states, 'It ought to be easy to use enlarged text on the blackboard, on sheets handed out or in PowerPoint presentations, but they don't do this'. This illuminates how even the simplest things can either promote or inhibit participation, but the importance of clearly distributed responsibilities are needed, even for the smallest details.

From an AT centre's perspective, cooperation with local schools and teachers varies a great deal. While they find some teachers very interested and eager to learn, they find others quite reluctant, with apparent mental blocks when it comes to technology. AT centres also experience the cooperation with teachers as dependent on the teachers' working culture, what subject or discipline the teacher belongs to or the workplace milieu into which the teacher is socialised. Last but not least, AT centres find the frames and structures under which the teachers work influence whether the teachers are able to employ AT (Söderström 2012). Teachers' working conditions not only influence their teaching, but equally influence students' learning and their opportunities to participate and be included. In particular, how a school is managed is of vital importance in this respect (Wendelborg 2010; Wendelborg and Kvello 2010; Wendelborg and Tøssebro 2010).

According to Tronsmo (2010), school management has an indirect impact on teachers' level of ambition, the educational setting, norms and culture, and the school's collaborative relationships with external partners (Tronsmo 2010). While

some schools have only a few special needs students, other schools have more. However, it appears that deliberate and positive focus on issues of individual adaptation and full inclusion of all students by school management is always a prerequisite for special needs students' participation in regular classroom activities (Bekken 2009; Tronsmo 2010; Söderström 2012). Kermit et al. (2014) conclude that as a social institution, the school has failed in its mission as an inclusive institution. They identify three problem areas: the need for adequate knowledge/competence, established special educational practices and the need for innovative thinking about inclusion (Kermit et al. 2014). However, on a micro level – at an individual school or in an individual classroom – this picture may be more complex and varied.

One teacher in the current study explains, 'The management is very good at facilitating individual adaptation. When a visually impaired student attended our school, the management told me to let them know if I needed anything special to adapt my teaching to this particular pupil'. In other words, this management was not only aware of this student's special needs but was also very forthcoming and benevolent in its efforts to include this student in the ordinary school setting. Consequently, the visually impaired student received all her teaching in the regular classroom setting together with her classmates. Moreover, all teachers conducting this particular class were carefully chosen according to their ability to be flexible, creative and innovative.

At other schools, however, the school management may limit disabled students' opportunities to participate and be included. Universal design and individual adaptation for pupils with special needs may not be considered. Another teacher states, 'The school management does not have a clue about disabled students' rights', referring to the Education Act of 1997, which proclaims that all children have the right to attend their local school and a regular class or group within this local school (Education Act 1997).

Bekken (2009) found that when it comes to exclusion of blind and partially sighted students, school management's poor competence and lack of follow-up on all levels is usually the culprit. This trend is in strong contrast to the inclusive ideology of the Norwegian Education Act (1997) and other public documents in this area. Additionally, this trend illustrates that regardless of the potential AT holds for disabled students, the technology alone does not enhance participation in ordinary school settings. The triggering factor for full utilisation of AT's anticipated benefits is released when socio-material practices are incorporated in regular classroom settings in mainstream schools.

Concluding remarks

This chapter has revealed how practical details and situations reflect attitudes and competencies, and how they make a difference in disabled students' everyday school life. However, one of the greatest obstacles to making education truly inclusive is a persistent deficit perspective on disability and subsequent individualisation of disabled students' education (Gable 2013; Lalvani 2013). Changing teaching strategies to include adaptations for individual students naturally and in all aspects of classroom activities is not an easy task. Before reaching natural inclusion of all pupils in mainstream school settings, constant awareness of this issue is required from school management and teachers.

While socio-material practices of AT use in the classroom are intended to facilitate disabled students' participation, inattentive or unintentional moments of non-use place disabled students in social isolation. These constant shifts between AT use and non-use characterise the socio-material practices of regular classroom activities in mainstream schools. Disabled students in need of AT who attend mainstream schools are thus exposed to a constant flow between social participation and social isolation during one and the same lesson or school day. Further research should investigate the consequences, educational and social, of this constant flow. If the educational system is to be truly inclusive, change that brings practice closer to ideology is needed. This involves an inclusive turn, that is, addressing and challenging the perceptions and thinking behind management and practice.

5 Information and communication technologies

The social envelope of young people's everyday lives

[handwritten annotations: "See markers + useful for social/personal chapter - some's relevant to ethic."]

[handwritten annotation in left margin: "gender?"]

In many western countries, political policy aims to secure an information society for all by emphasising how important it is that everybody, including the disabled, is able to use information and communication technology (ICT) (e-Norway 2009; Helsper 2011). Achieving this goal necessitates making ICT accessible *and* usable in light of each individual person's needs and preferences. However, despite laws intended to promote online access for all, disabled people continue to have limited access due to inaccessible design and implementation of websites and other digital technologies (Vicente and Lòpez 2010; Jaeger 2012). Furthermore, there are concerns that increasing Internet penetration will exacerbate digital inequalities among young people and that exclusion from digital networks will be a severely damaging exclusion, especially for vulnerable and marginalised subgroups of young people (Livingstone and Helsper 2007). To be marginalised is to be put aside and not accounted for, not recognised and made unessential (Goffman 1963). One subgroup of vulnerable and marginalised young people is young disabled people (Wendelborg 2010).

This chapter investigates how young disabled people are exposed to digital differentiation, how such differentiation involves more than technological access alone and how differentiation affects possibilities for inclusion in the peer group. Digital differentiation refers to differences in ICT use among those with equal ICT access and the social implications of these differences. Digital differentiation is conceptualised as a dynamic phenomenon, and adoption and use of ICT is interpreted as a social phenomenon (Peter and Valkenburg 2006; Yu 2006; Vaage 2008). The chapter draws on data previously publicised in the journal *Future Internet* (Söderström 2013).

The Internet-connected computer is a social medium that illuminates emerging differentiations among young people. The chapter describes how such differentiations emerge through technological shortcomings and social anticipations, especially anticipations and stereotypes of disability and of assistive ICT. Greater knowledge of these conditions is vitally important for providing usable assistive ICT that meets young disabled peoples' preferences.

While the Internet's potential benefits have grown, especially in recent decades, equality of access has not improved correspondingly (Jaeger 2012). A digital differentiation perspective usually perceives user characteristics as more influential on ICT adoption than the technology's characteristics. However, the field of disability studies finds that for young disabled people, the characteristics of the technology itself are vital for providing or inhibiting access to the Internet and thus to participation in the digital information society (Söderström and Ytterhus 2010; Vicente and Lòpez 2010; Jaeger 2012). Digital differentiations, however, are neither technological nor social, but relational, that is, a mutual interaction between the technology, the person and the social context. Thus, ICT and the digital world have become an intervening catalyst in people's social spheres.

Before elaborating on these issues, brief insight into previous research in this field as well as the chapter's theoretical departure point are provided. The chapter's closing discussion expands on technology's significance to young people's negotiations of impairment and to common perceptions of disability.

The social envelope of young people's everyday lives

The potential effect of ICT on young people's lives has to be studied in its social envelope, which includes the sets of expectations, contexts and social practices that surround it. Postmodern adolescence is a life phase in which new codes and implied understandings are acquired, where the self is situated in a social context and where individual meaning is created. In this life stage, young people spend an increasing amount of time with peers, friends become ever more significant and friendship relations are voluntary, equal and multiple (Bø and Schiefloe 2007).

Young people are generally curious and enthusiastic about technology. They easily incorporate new technologies into their everyday lives, and young people value ICT in particular (Buckingham 2006; McMillan and Morrison 2006). In addition, most young people are active computer and Internet users. Online communication and surfing the Internet for leisure are the most popular digital activities among young people in general (McMillan and Morrison 2006; Kaare, Brantzæg, Heim and Endestad 2007; Räsänen and Kouvo 2007). A comprehensive body of research has found that young people's online communication use and activities are highly integrated into their offline relationships; it has also found that the local world and the digital world are no longer separate worlds, but rather are permeable and influence each other (Buckingham 2006; Söderström 2009).

While adolescents' socio-economic and cognitive resources shape their use of the Internet as an information or entertainment medium, such differences are less clear-cut for adolescents' use of the Internet as a social medium. Previous socio-economic differences related to young people's ICT use have evened out, especially when it comes to the Internet as a social medium (Peter and Valkenburg 2006; Livingstone and Helsper 2007; Näslund and Gardelli 2013). However, young people are expected by their peers to be digitally connected, and if they are not, they are unable to participate fully in their peers' communities (McMillan and Morrison 2006; Söderström and Ytterhus 2010; Söderström 2012).

Young disabled people are first and foremost ordinary young people with the same desires, aspirations and needs for companionship, recognition and belonging as other young people. Adolescence is a particularly challenging and sensitive period for all young people, when values, attitudes and identity develop and settle. Disabled youth frequently encounter challenges in their peer relationships during this time. Such challenges can include physical accessibility, individual attitudes or social anticipations towards disabled people. Thus, young disabled people who adopt assistive ICT seek to make the technology coherent with their own preferred self-identity (Söderström 2009; Söderström and Ytterhus 2010).

Previous research on disabled people and ICT has mainly focused on adults' perceptions and use of ICT. Past work in this area illuminates how disabled adults, especially those who have difficulty meeting others, benefit from online self-help groups and disability-related websites (Cummings, Kiesler and Sproull 2002; Seymour and Lupton 2004; Seymour 2005). Though disability and kinship remain the principle online bonds for disabled adults, the possibilities the Internet offers have great personal significance for many disabled people (Vicente and Lòpez 2010; Jaeger 2012). However, in line with other studies, the category age shows the most consistent difference in use of ICT (Vaage 2008; Söderström 2009). This chapter illuminates digital differences within the adolescent age category.

A theory of information worlds

The theory of information worlds is a conceptual framework designed for understanding the information behaviour of specific populations within a broader society. In building this framework, Burnett and Jaeger (2008) drew on two sets of theoretical concepts: the macro-level concept of Habermas (1989) related to life-worlds, and the micro-level concept of Chatman (1999) related to small-worlds. These two concepts are seen as complementary tools for providing a better approach to investigating access and exchange of information in society.

The theory of information worlds describes different levels of access to information, and to ICT and the Internet. These levels of access are (i) physical access to the technology, (ii) intellectual access to the content of information and (iii) social access to interaction. All three levels of access are required for inclusion. While most research on disability and ICT has focused on physical access issues, Jaeger (2012) points out that social access is the most advanced level of access and the most important to inclusion. This chapter investigates the significance of both physical and social access, especially young disabled people's experiences of physical access intervening with social access. By examining the different levels of access, the theory of information worlds also focuses on five social elements. This chapter focuses on two of these elements: (i) *social norms*, a group's shared sense of the appropriateness of social appearances and behaviours, and (ii) *social types*, the roles that define actors and how they are perceived within a group (Jaeger 2012).

To illustrate how digital differences are more than a matter of access, this conceptual framework is applied in an investigation of how physical access intervenes with social access, and how this influences young disabled people's interaction in their peer group.

Digital differentiation – More than a matter of access

Using ICT and assistive ICT entails more than gaining access or overcoming practical barriers. For young people, ICT use is significant as a means of self-representation and a strategy of distinction. In this strategy of distinction, being perceived by the peer group as ordinary stands out as most important to young disabled persons (Söderström and Ytterhus 2010; Asbjørnslett 2015). The question is how digital differentiation influences young disabled people's possibilities in terms of distinction within their peer group. To answer this question, data from two qualitative studies are investigated: one study of 11 visually impaired young people ages 15–20, and one of 12 young people with movement difficulties ages 15–20. The main findings related to digital differentiation are illustrated with some examples that are typical for the experiences and statements of these young disabled persons.

When physical access is hampered

Sometimes little things have serious consequences, as when physical access to technology is hampered by technological errors or deficiencies. Lisa is a 15-year-old girl with severe mobility difficulties. Due to a fair amount of involuntary upper limb movements, it is strenuous for her to control her finger movements to hit the right key on the computer's keyboard. Thus, she has been assigned a BigKeys, an enlarged computer keyboard. Lisa enjoys writing, but sometimes it is exhausting and annoying. Lisa explains:

> When the letter 'A' is not working, I get quite annoyed. The lack of this little 'A' gives me problems in chatting with friends, and I miss out on a lot of what is going on. The AT equipment just has to work. Why don't they check this at the assistive technology centre before delivering it? Do they not expect me to need the letter 'A'? What do they think I use the computer for? It is vital that all the assistive ICT just works all the time.

Here Lisa describes the consequences that a little technical error might have. Lisa has physical access to her computer, but due to a technical error, the missing letter A, she lacks social access to her peer group's digital interaction. The rare teenager who is not constantly online is isolated from his or her peers, says Jaeger (2012). Moreover, an AT device's impact on the user's activity and social participation reflects its usability (Arthanat, Bauer, Lenker, Nochajski and Wu 2007). To have a high level of usability, AT must reduce physical, cognitive and linguistic effort and promote convenience, efficiency and productivity. Even more importantly, AT must support social norms and types within the peer group (Ravneberg 2009).

Eve is a 15-year-old partially sighted girl who has been allocated a screen magnifier software application for her computer. As long as the assistive ICT works, all goes well, but as soon as one thing malfunctions, everything falls apart. Eve depends on her assistive ICT tools for all her digital activities. When an error occurs with the assistive ICT, the assistive technology centre is responsible for repairs (Svendsen 2010). Eve says:

> It feels like it takes years from the time we send in the assistive equipment to the assistive technology centre until it is repaired. In the meantime, I must do without this equipment, and this has major consequences for my social life. I get so tired of waiting for the assistive technology centre to do their job. And it's a little hard to complain, too, because I am really grateful for all the help I get. But it is a big thing that is missing, and I am totally dependent on it.

That things take a long time to be deal with is something most users of AT have experienced, especially when it comes to assistive ICT equipment maintenance. Many users of this sort of equipment and various service providers in the municipalities have confirmed this (Svendsen 2010). However, to be included and acknowledged in their peer group, young disabled people are completely dependent on their ICT tools being operational at all times.

AT that does not work as needed creates frustrations that often lead users to reject the technologies (Arthanat et al. 2007; Söderström and Ytterhus 2010). Children and young people have an especially low tolerance for technical errors or deficiencies that are detrimental to their social appearances and position in their peer group. When young disabled people encounter such technical barriers, they experience a disruption with their group's social norms and feel that their impairment is put front stage (Söderström and Ytterhus 2010). Tore, a 17-year-old boy with fine motor difficulties, describes BigKeys in this way:

> It is all right when it works. But when it doesn't work, I easily get annoyed. Then there are so many spelling errors, and people think I can't spell because I am disabled when it really is the BigKeys that doesn't work.

When technical barriers occur, young disabled people believe that their peers can easily define them as disabled and that they have failed to meet the group's norm. Consequently, they feel that assistive ICT carries inherent stereotypes of disability and marks them as disabled. As a result, many young disabled persons avoid using assistive ICT, especially in interactions with friends and peers. As long as they have a choice, most of them will choose to manage without assistive ICT because they experience its use as a barrier to displaying themselves as valued actors according to the group's shared sense of appropriate appearance and behaviour. However, many of these young people have no choice if they want to participate and be included in their immediate group.

When physical access is available, but technologies are incompatible

Sometimes the assistive ICT works just fine but is incompatible with other ICT devices, at least for user's purposes. Eivind is a 17-year-old visually impaired boy who has been allocated a screen magnifier for his computer. Eivind's experience with the screen magnifier is quite similar to that of other young visually impaired persons. Eivind says, 'I think the screen magnifier is too much hassle. It doesn't always provide access to the sites I want to visit anyway. I try to manage without it'. In Eivind's experience, the screen magnifier splits up text and misses graphics, making it difficult for him to keep up with his friends' online interactions, especially when they play computer games. Another visually impaired person is 17-year-old Iselin. She presents herself as an outgoing person and talks a great deal about how she uses the computer for social interaction. She explains,

> Some websites are very difficult to read, especially websites with a lot of graphics. Sometimes I try to access a website a hundred times, and if it is something important or some really good stuff, then I have to find a nice, patient soul who will read it to me.

Even with such AT devices as screen readers and Talks, websites with graphic elements are challenging for visually impaired persons to access. However, websites containing videos and graphic elements are very popular among young people and are often a central conversation topic.

Many young visually impaired people recount numerous encounters with inaccessible ICT and describe unusable assistive ICT. Unusable assistive ICT does not necessarily mean that the assistive ICT is faulty in itself; it means that the technology cannot be used for these young people's intended purposes. These purposes are typically digital interactions on the micro level with friends and peers, most often on websites containing graphics. Such encounters illuminate the intertwined and mutually permeable nature of a digitized life-world and people's social interactions within their own small-worlds. Furthermore, these encounters reveal how obstacles in one world affect the other as well. The ability to act and participate in small-world settings with friends is vital to enable young people to meet their peer group's social norms. Losing the ability to participate in such settings means young visually impaired people cannot meet their peer group's social norms. They then risk being perceived as deviant and ascribed a social identity as disabled. Thus, as a result of incompatible technology, a digital differentiation emerges, excluding young people with visual impairments from the small-world of their peer group.

Most people are unaware of the technological possibilities AT enables and do not expect visually impaired people to be able to browse websites. Furthermore, anticipations of what disabled people can and cannot do are often determined by a notion of disability as an individual, medical condition, leading to the perception that a disability constitutes a person's primary status, thus neglecting his or her other qualities (Kent and Smith 2006; Ravneberg 2009). Social anticipations lead many young disabled persons to work much harder than others to prove their capabilities and competencies, even when these capabilities and competencies are unconnected to their impairments. The next section illuminates how such social anticipations can cause digital differentiations within a peer group.

Social access to interaction requires more than just physical access

Perceptions and experiences of what is real, social and interpersonal shift contemporaneously with expansion of the arenas in which communications, interactions and relationships occur. As a result, people's small-world on the micro level and life-world on the macro level are no longer separate entities, but are permeable, mutually constituted and embedded within everyday life. Young people in particular are exposed to the permeability of these two worlds. They are expected to be digitally connected, and if they are not, they are unable to act and participate with their peers within their small-world. Such availability is described as 'always-on' relationships (Kaare et al. 2007). Such relationships are characterised by the need and demand for constant connection and by dependency on ever-accessible and ever-usable technology. This describes young people's relationships today. However, little is yet known about how this state of affairs affects the small-worlds of those who are not 'always-on'.

Kristin is a 16-year-old girl with movement difficulties. Although she has been allocated both the BigKeys and MyTobi AT devices, she does not use her computer very often. BigKeys is a computer keyboard with extra-large keys, and MyTobi is an eye-tracking communication technology for people with linguistic difficulties and/or severe fine motor skill difficulties. Kristin says,

> Well, actually I don't use [BigKeys] that much. I have some trouble hitting the right keys, and it takes forever to use MyTobi. It's a little bit annoying because all my friends are on the Web.

Christine, a 19 year-old girl with movement difficulties, puts it this way:

> I think it is easier to talk to people face to face than on the Web. On the Web I easily get confused. It is a little bit difficult to keep track of everything that's happening. So I don't have the habit of chatting online.

Gaining social access to interactions is experienced differently by different users and in different contexts. For many young disabled persons, gaining social access to interactions is associated with difficulties, confusion and exertion, even when physical access to technology is secured. Due to ICT's central role in young people's social interactions, those who encounter barriers to it are particularly disadvantaged in their social relationships. Encountering these barriers causes young disabled people to feel that their impairment is on display, and this is something they strongly want to avoid.

While youth is commonly perceived as symbolic of hope, vigour and strength, disability is commonly perceived as symbolic of tragedy, invalidity and frailty (Hughes, Russell and Paterson 2005). Moreover, when young people perceive certain technology as outside the norm, or if the technology overtly signals impairment, use of such technology has to be either disguised or negated. When using AT is an option but not an 'enforced choice', young people's definitions of what constitutes normality seem to be the principal factor in determining whether they are willing to use the technology (Ravneberg 2009; Söderström and Ytterhus 2010).

Two visually impaired boys, Stig and Jon, deem their assistive ICT unsuitable. Stig, who is 15, says that he prefers to enlarge characters on the screen in the ordinary way, 'like everybody else', and Jon, who is 16, does not think he needs the assistive ICT. Thus, they find that the AT and mainstream ICT are incompatible. Furthermore, they negate the significance of their impairment by emphasising the importance of using mainstream ICT. Even though screen magnifiers provide partially sighted persons better physical access to the web's visual interfaces, most young partially sighted persons find this AT incompatible with their preferred way of using ICT. When they describe their experiences with assistive ICT, feelings of restriction, difference and dependency emerge, reflected in expressions that typify their perceptions of the assistive ICT: 'too much bother', 'no point' and 'stupid', 'difficult', 'boring' and 'annoying'. Not surprisingly, young people's vocabulary differs from that of adults and academics. Their expressions reflect a sense of assistive ICT as something that draws attention to restriction, difference and dependency, characteristics that are associated with a medical understanding of disability and with a deviant identity (Ravneberg 2009) – an identity that almost all young disabled persons rejected (Söderström and Ytterhus 2010; Asbjørnslett 2015).

However, some young disabled persons, such as young blind persons, who are totally dependent on a screen reader, or persons with upper limb movement difficulties, who are dependent on the BigKeys keyboard, do not have the luxury of rejecting assistive ICT if they want to participate in their small-world with friends. The vital importance of such participation forces them to adopt the assistive ICT. Even though using AT identifies them as disabled, it is also their only opportunity to participate. In such cases, this opportunity seems to overshadow the risk of being identified as disabled.

Moreover, disability is not an issue for young disabled persons; their impairment is a natural part of their everyday lives. When young disabled persons are directly questioned about how they experience their impairment, they typically answer, 'I do what ordinary people do, hang out with friends', 'It's nothing' and 'I just talk to my friends like everybody else about everyday stuff'. When discussing impairment, it is not uncommon for most young disabled persons to demonstrate reticence (Söderström and Ytterhus 2010; Asbjørnslett 2015). These young people do not perceive themselves as different from their peers just because they happen to have an impairment. Today's young disabled people construct their self-identity in such a way that impairment is negated as an identifier. These young people demonstrate how ICT use involves more than access to technical equipment: use of the appropriate technology and the way in which it is used are of equal importance. Thus, many young disabled persons find AT and mainstream ICT, which are compatible on a literal level, incompatible for their preferred use.

Young disabled people find themselves caught in a bind between concealment and disclosure. In a culture of consumption, the symbols of youth and disability exist in profound tension with one another, as do ICT and AT (Hughes et al. 2005;

Ravneberg 2009; Söderström and Ytterhus 2010). Thus, youth and disability, like mainstream ICT and assistive ICT, constitute two very distinct and incompatible identities that clash with and recoil from one another. The incompatibility of youth and disability makes it even more difficult for young disabled people to negotiate a preferred self-identity. Even though using assistive ICT may ease their access to ICT and their social interactions within the small-world of their peer group, it also discloses their impairment. This disclosure makes them feel revealed as deviant and disabled, an identity from which they distance themselves. Young disabled persons are routinely confronted with this dilemma of concealment or disclosure, as they find themselves forced to trade maximal social inclusion by using mainstream ICT for improved empowerment and employing assistive ICT for improved participation.

Concluding remarks

The majority of young people will adopt and utilise any communication tool at their disposal, and their use of the Internet is increasingly communicative: it is a place to build networks, display identity and interact socially (Söderström 2009; Vicente and Lòpez 2010; Jaeger 2012). This creates permeability between the micro-level small-world and the macro-level life-world.

For young disabled people, this permeability also involves dependency on accessible and usable AT that can enable interaction with peers at any time and place. The allocation of such AT, however, may give rise to the confident assumption that the goal of access has been achieved when physical access to the AT has been provided. This confidence may neglect the reality that young disabled people face and leave them at a dead end. Consequently, one may be fooled to assume that assistive ICT evens out digital differentiations, when it actually may facilitate the opposite.

Most AT is reactive in design, and mainstream technology will have moved another step forward by the time accommodations are made. If mainstream technologies were universally designed from the outset, the time gap between the availability of new technology and the availability of suitable AT could be eliminated. However, universal design is not a panacea for making ICT accessible for disabled people. The complexity of the digitized environment and differences in how people access and use ICT may represent an unsolvable problem for universal design's goals. Thus, continuous development of usable AT is both necessary and complementary to universal design, and this development needs to become more innovative and proactive in its approach. Moreover, AT's impact on the user's self-identity needs to be carefully considered by both developers and providers of AT.

The most significant implication of digital differentiation for young disabled persons relates to different technologies' effects on users being perceived as ordinary young people and their ability to enable social interaction in their small-world with peers. This phenomenon underlines the importance of the relationship between universal design and AT, and the need for compatibility between the two. Assistive

ICT will always assist mainstream, pre-existing ICT. The challenge is to make assistive ICT sufficiently flexible to be innovative and proactive and to consider carefully this technology's inherent symbolic values and impact on social roles and norms. This chapter has illustrated how small technical errors and deficiencies, incompatible technologies and the permeability of the macro life-world and micro small-world create digital differences in the subgroup of vulnerable youth by putting impairment on display, thus reproducing stereotypes of disability. Further research in this field must investigate how assistive ICT can become more easily adaptable to individual users' requirements.

6 Usability and aesthetics of assistive technologies

This chapter deals with the perspectives of adult users on the usability of AT. The term *consumption junction* is used as an analytic concept. The consumption junction is a network seen from the *inside* out, as Cowan (2012) describes it. The network consists of public service providers, private vendors, producers, suppliers, designers, health professionals and several other actors. The network is seen from the subjective user's point of view or from the end-user's point of view, which is a widely used term for describing the actual receiver of AT services. In this book the term *user* is preferred over the term *end-user*, as described in Chapter 7.

In this chapter and the following one, the user is located in the midst of the web or network. The user is at the centre of the network, not the designer, producer, buyer or purchaser. This point of departure means that questions of user identities and user strategies of distinctions are important to discuss. The consumption junction is the actual interface where technological diffusion occurs and where technologies start to reorganise social structures (Cowan 2012:255). In this chapter, we ask: Which paths do users find worthwhile to pursue? What are their strategies of distinctions and how are social structures reorganised? What elements stand out as being more important than others? What are reasons for non-use and/or abandonment? What are the risks and hazards attached to this? An intersectional perspective is also applied in the chapter, as disability is not the only category dealt with, but also gender, age and lifestyle. The intersectional perspective proposes, as outlined in Chapter 1, that one single identity category (such as disabled), cannot be used as the only analytical frame without exploring how issues of other identity categories additionally come to bear on the person's experience. In this chapter, users are seen as multidimensional and uniquely whole (Samuels and Ross-Sheriff 2008).

Usability, utility and identity

First, we turn to the concept of usability. What is usability, and how can we distinguish between usability and utility? For many users utility (functionality) comes first. Next it is important that the product looks good. For others it may be the other way around. Utility in combination with usability are both important dimensions for users. In this chapter, it is the users' perspectives on devices' *usability* that stands at the centre, and less so the devices' utility or effectiveness, even though it is difficult to separate these two dimensions.

What is usability? According to Wilson (2002), usability denotes user friendliness. It also implies some goodness of design. Often, it is used synonymously with 'user-friendly', 'easy to use' or 'easy to learn'. The International Organization for Standardization (ISO) has defined usability as follows: *The extent to which a product can be used by specified users to achieve specified goals with effectiveness (task completion by users), efficiency (task in time) and satisfaction (responded by user in term of experience) in a specified context of use* (ISO 9241–11). In contrast, utility is mainly concerned with what the product can do such as features, function and technologies.

Identity categories influence personal choices, experiences and reflections on devices. Disability is not the only identity category considered. This chapter discusses usability by focusing on aesthetics and design, without emphasising any particular disability, but focusing instead on the significance of lifestyle, gender and age in an intersectional perspective. Susan Wendell points out that describing disabled people or women as a social group 'might ignore and make invisible differences among them including differences of race, class, sexual identity, age, ethnicity and (dis)ability' (Wendell 1996:70). People in wheelchairs might see some similarities between themselves and people who are hard of hearing, yet still claim that they have little in common. Thus, we do not see disabled people as comprising an undifferentiated unitary group. Being disabled is not always the most important aspect of a person's identity or social position (Watson 2002). Identity is dynamic and derived from multiple sources (Jagger 2002).

Questions to be considered include how users think of wheelchair design and hearing instruments, and how they use them. In what ways are devices conceived of by young and old, female or male users, and how helpful do they think devices are for their ability to manage daily life? What strategies do people use when facing restricted choices in order to get a good match between themselves and the device? Abandonment is, of course, one choice, as we shall see in Chapter 7 with regard to adolescents. However, if users do not abandon the products, how do they cope? Do they conform to the design of the AT, or do they oppose it? Do they alter it, and, if so, how?

One thing is for certain: users have different interpretations and priorities. They use and talk about their technologies differently. To begin with, the 11 interviewees on whom this chapter is based (five men and six women between the ages of 22 and 68) want more choices within the national and local assortment of ATs available to them from the welfare state (Ravneberg 2009). They want a larger choice to allow for individuality and personality when selecting a new AT product. As we will see, matching people and AT devices is a very delicate and difficult task. Aesthetic appearances, for instance, are not a priority of the welfare state. A civil servant in the British Health Department clearly stated, 'In the UK the priority for each patient clearly is the clinical need rather than aesthetic appearance' (e-mail from the Health Department, 2007). Matching people and devices is more difficult than matching people and clothes. Surprisingly, people do not necessarily use devices they 'clinically' need. People abandon devices and do take risks.

The distinctive cyborg and different ways of understanding and using AT

Many users claim that the products they use are important body parts. 'The wheel-chair', according to Thomas, 'is an extension of my body. It is my legs'. David compares hearing devices and wheelchairs when he says, 'It is supposed to be a part of me. It is very important. The same goes for wheelchairs. It is not just any bike; it is more personal, isn't it?' The technologies become an integrated part of people's bodies if they are a good match. This interesting transgression of boundaries can be linked to Donna Haraway's (1991) cyborg image, or fiction of the human being. A cyborg is defined as an organism that adds to, or enhances its abilities by using technology. In her view, technologies are 'crucial tools recrafting our bodies' and 'enforcing new social relations' between people (Haraway 1991:164). Machines such as computers, mobile telephones, glasses, wheelchairs, hearing instruments and even pencils are all 'prosthetic devices', 'intimate components' or 'friendly selves' as Haraway describes them (p. 164).

Obviously, a device does not obtain such a 'friendly' status if the user does not want to use it. Many people abandon assistive devices, dismantle them or keep them in cupboards, drawers or closets, because they, for some reason, are not satisfied with them. David refused to install an alarm device in his flat even though he (clinically) needed it: 'In the flat where I live now, I have not installed it because it is not possible to have such ugly boxes all over the flat. It is still unpacked, lying nicely in the original box'. David has a clean style. He rejects installing devices that are (in his opinion) supposed to appeal to his grandmother: 'Then the product might end in a drawer or in a box'. Nevertheless, how can he manage *without* any signaling devices? He is after all entitled to one due to his hearing impairment. Is it not a big risk to take if he does not hear the alarm? David's answer to this question was that he was not sure and that he kept thinking of it, but that the design stopped him.

> On the other side, I think that if it gets a fire or something like that, will I notice the smoke alarm in the hall? Will I notice it in the bedroom when I am sleeping? For those vital things, it could be wise to have one anyway despite its ugliness. I have been thinking of mounting it for that use and not for the others. Then it is the design again. You cannot have, if you try to have a style in a place and then there are being installed many ugly boxes that do not belong. All those things have a box; in addition, some of them have a thing like that (adapter), and they must have electricity some of them. Some work on batteries, others need electricity, and then you need an adaptor and then . . . At the same time, the trend is that you are not supposed to have so many boxes. They collect a lot of dust. Why are we supposed to have all those boxes?

It is important to many users that the product looks good. On a device both looking good and functioning well, Thomas, a young wheelchair user, notes, 'You are lucky if those two fit together. I want to see the whole selection, to pick a bit of Invacare and a bit of Handicare. I want the chair to fit me. It must be made for me only'. Thomas says that products must not make people feel less normal. Nor must they make people more disabled than they are: 'That is how it becomes with some of the aids. It feels like having a big clumsy thing on you. You lose your self-confidence more than if it had been a fancy product. It should be something you are proud to show to others'.

Very often people do not have much choice if they want to be active. How do they cope if they think the devices they have are not usable or are not 'friendly selves'? One solution is, of course, to use it as little as possible. Another strategy is to replace the device with other products, as Alan does. Alan has a standard folding manual wheelchair. He uses it at airports, shopping centres, the university, cafeterias and the cinema. He also has a car that he uses very often. In addition, he uses crutches. He says that he is not dependent on his wheelchair and indicates that it is his own choice to use it. He has chosen to be more dependent on his car and his crutches. He does not want to be dependent on the wheelchair because he finds it stigmatising. Alan can walk with crutches, but it is not easy for him. He resists using the wheelchair even though several times he has been offered a better one by the service provider in the municipality. He does not bother to have a smarter wheelchair. Using a wheelchair is to him a symbol of disability, and he does not look upon himself as disabled. The wheelchair he uses is just a 'stand-in' device. It is to be used in places where he cannot use the car or the crutches. He has no personal relationship to the wheelchair. It is not a 'friendly self' to him, but a stigmatised means of transportation. Having a smart wheelchair would be a defeat for him, signaling that he is disabled.

The same view is also applicable in understanding mechanisms in the hearing aid market. That hearing impairment is something to hide, and that flesh-coloured instruments are preferable, has for a long time been the main message in this market. Many people adjust themselves to this message. Wearing colourful hearing instruments or wearing them as jewels, like wearing designer glasses, is not preferable according to this marketing message. Eva, a woman in her late thirties, is one among many who confirm this interpretation of hearing devices. She does not want her hearing instruments to be 'cool'. She prefers them to be as discreet as possible. Using hearing instruments is stigmatising, she says: 'It is because people might think of you only as a person who is hard of hearing, and not as the person you actually are, who also has a hearing loss. You are composed of more than a handicap'. She claims that wearing visible hearing instruments gives you a master status as disabled. It was a personal capitulation for her when she had to wear two hearing instruments instead of one, and it was a long process to make this change. Now she has two skin-coloured digital hearing instruments in the ear and is quite happy with them. What she really does not like to use at all, however, is the tele coil technology around her neck as she finds it too ugly to wear; therefore, she has abandoned it. She would have considered using it if it had been designed as a necklace. Thus, Eva would like hearing instruments to be designed as jewelry to emphasise her femininity. She wants them to be discreet. She claims that flesh-coloured instruments visualise her disability less than colourful ones.

From this, we can conclude that AT largely represents distinctions of identities in the same way as many other products in 'ordinary' markets. The discourse in the AT market, however, is different, as it also reflects traditional ways of thinking about medical cure, treatment and rehabilitation. The history of the wheelchair and how it has been interpreted over time illustrates a change from seeing it as a failure or as a personal tragedy to seeing it as a recrafting of the body in the cyborg way or as a liberating personal part of the body. Using 'wheeled chairs' was at the end of the nineteenth century often interpreted as a sign of failure of medicine to find a cure. It could also be interpreted as an individual sign of failure or weakness – that the person had failed, or had given up on rehabilitation (Woods and Watson 2004).

Many authors have pointed out that the influence of the medical model has resulted in people viewing wheelchairs as symbols of a personal tragedy. This might be part of the explanation as to why Alan, Eva and many others find AT devices stigmatising and reject using them as long as possible. This discourse postulates that using a wheelchair or a hearing aid limits people's participation and possibilities. Hiding hearing loss can thus be seen as an expression of traditional ways of thinking about people with hearing impairment as being 'dumb'. This is of particular significance in the labour market. To a young man like Alan or a young woman like Eva, the message within this medical discourse is that it is important to hang on to your crutches as long as possible or hide your hearing aid if you want entrance into the job market.

The other five wheelchair users in the study indicated that a wheelchair is a *very* personal matter; it is something you wear. As Louise explained,

> I 'dress' my wheelchair every morning. I am not 'chained' to it. If one uses that metaphor it becomes negative regarding the function my chair is supposed to have. I am dressing it. It does that my radius of action and my quality of life reach a maximum level. At the same time, I want my chair to be as little dominating as possible in relation to the person I want to be.

The aesthetics of the wheelchair are thus very important to these users. They can even be more important than its functionality. Thomas said that he would probably not use the chair if he was not given the choice to decide its design and composition down to the smallest detail. He wanted the chair for outdoor use as stripped (without handbrakes, push handles, armrests and so on) as possible and with clean lines. He wanted a chair for really rough outdoor use, like a mountain bike. He chose a black manual active chair for outdoor use and at work, and another, differently designed manual chair at home. His passion was the rims for outdoor use. After several years, he had found *his* rims on the Internet. He had bought them himself, as they were not available through the public service provision, nor was there any information about them: 'When I found the new rims, I sat down in another similar wheelchair without those rims. I looked at it and thought that, yes, this is me; this is definitely much more me than before'. The rims were black and aesthetically pleasing, like car rims. One of the rims was decorated with a minia-ture silver skull. The decoration can be compared to a skin tattoo – a kind of body modification symbolising something meaningful or important for the individual who wears it. Together, the wheelchair and the person in it 'radiated' strong powers because of the silver skull on the rim.

Julie, age 50, said that her manual and electric wheelchairs are as important to her as pairs of shoes are to non-wheelchair users. She said that she wanted her wheelchairs to be neutral, black or grey all over. She wanted her chairs to match her clothes, just like shoes do. She did not want her wheelchairs to come in 'screaming' colours or in several colours. If they did, it would be terrible, and she would personally redecorate it in black immediately. Her chairs had to be neutral so that she could dress in colourful clothes. She did not want people to pay atten-tion to the wheelchair but to her. She wanted to make a nice impression with her body. The manual wheelchair was more important to her than the electric one as it signaled less dependency. She could, in fact, use one of her feet. In addition, the manual chair was smaller and easier to manoeuver indoors than the electric one. She used the manual wheelchair indoors, at work, on airplanes and when travel-ling, and used the electric one outdoors, for shopping and walking. She never used the electric chair indoors. If she did, she stated that she 'would feel like an elephant in a glass house'. She could, in fact, manage short distances without the electric one.

The AT products are in this perspective not seen as a failure, as postulated by traditional interpretations within the medical discourse, but as representations of selves. This way of seeing and using AT, however, is not widely understood, and for the users it had taken years of struggle with public service providers to get there. First, it takes time to get what one needs from service providers. Second, it takes time to adapt to using a wheelchair or a hearing instrument. Thomas said: 'I understand if people get tired after a year. As I said, I still struggle after ten years. After ten years, I still struggle with cushions and things. Really, I shouldn't spend more time than a minute on this'. The majority of the service providers are not customer-oriented but patient-oriented. Henriette, who lost her hearing as an adult, stated,

> It should be the doctors informing us. My impression is that it is the users who are the experts. It is we, the users that find out about things; we are finding out stuff. It should really have been the other way around! It should be the doctor saying to me, 'But Henriette, you should know that this and that is on the market. I want you to try this and that'. But it is me who says, 'Why can't I try that? Isn't that good?' Then they answer, 'Yes, but I don't really . . . maybe you can try it on . . .' If you don't find out for yourself, you don't get to know anything!

Ian, a man in his 40s who uses electric wheelchairs, experienced a change in his life when he got a new electric wheelchair. The shift of chair changed his identity and his relationship to his wheelchair. Previously he could not distinguish between his body and his electric wheelchair. He used to have a very big electric wheelchair in which his body became very small. When he shaved himself, he could only see whether he was shaved or not, he could not see the match between his body and his chair. Now he had a new black and much smaller, smarter chair designed as an office chair. Ian stated, 'What they see when they see me, is me and not the chair. Before it used to be the other way around; the chair was so much *bigger* than me'. Getting a new chair had given him a new self-image. The distinction between his body and the wheelchair became clearer. He realised that he had become more attractive. He used two identical electric chairs for indoors, at work, as well as for outdoor use. They were elegant and had a modern office-like look. 'If the chair stops, I stop', he said. This was the reason for having two chairs. Besides being back-ups for each other, their new smarter design had transformed and transcended his identity.

David, a young man in his 20s, uses a flesh-coloured behind-the-ear product. Most of his life he had worn a hearing instrument that was as invisible as possible. He had also tried to avoid wearing it at all. Now he was ready to try on a more colourful product, such as a metal-coloured one. A few years ago, he would not have liked to have a hearing product that was visible. Now he didn't bother about that anymore. He had matured, he said. He reckoned that the product would be visible anyway, flesh-coloured or not, as it had to be behind the ear, so why not have a colourful one, he asked. Another reason he referred to was that many people are wearing ear technologies today: 'It is more accepted to wear a silver-coloured product, like a Bluetooth headset'. David thought that it would be cool to wear a silver-coloured product. Now he was ready for a product that expresses his identity, as a busy, young, hard-working man with great knowledge of technology, including modern digital hearing technology.

Tom, a 23-year-old man, has just started to wear hearing instruments on a permanent basis even though he had had a hearing loss since he was a child. Previously he wanted them always to be flesh-coloured, but now he had come out of the closet, so to speak. Something had changed within him too. His new hearing products are black and silver, and he is very happy with them. On the question of why he no longer wanted flesh-coloured devices, he answered that he associated those with old age:

> No, now I'm thinking that they look like instruments for people who are retired. Before, I didn't think like that at all. Before I used to think that this is how it is supposed to be. Now I think that these instruments that I have now, are more youth appealing or look newer, they are a little bit more designed than those old flesh coloured ones.

In sum, the choices of these users can be seen as examples of users being in opposition to traditional ways of seeing AT within the discourse of the medical model. Most of the users in this study are more or less recasting the AT out of its clinical functional limitations and towards a sense of self and social identity in a cultural context.

AT language displaying gender identities

Julia's chairs, and especially her manual chair, represent her femininity, ability and personality, she claims. Thus, they do not represent her disability, she states. The language Julia uses when talking about design is the language of tailors: 'My chairs are tailored around my body', she says. To borrow other chairs, as one has to do at airports or at shopping malls, is like using someone else's shoes. While Julia wants her chairs to be small, light-weight, elegant and nice to look at, reflecting her identity as a woman, Thomas wants his to be clean and easy, rough and tough, signaling strength and courage, like a car. His language is different, comparing his wheelchair to mountain bikes and cars more than clothes.

As to the question of whether the users want more gendered products, like a wheelchair specially designed for women, it turned out that half of the interviewees had not given this question a thought. A few of them nodded and said that yes, there are gender differences within AT products. It is a paradox that this question came as a surprise, as all of the interviewees (except two) saw their AT devices as intimate personal belongings, as a garment with which they struggled to get a better match. For them, the wheelchair was more than as a mere means of transportation. However, they think of the devices as more or less unisex. The eldest woman and man – Ian and Louise – are exceptions. Louise says that she is convinced that electric wheelchairs in particular are gendered: 'Of course, it is gendered! All of them are masculine. They are all big and monstrous, and fit best a man! To put a slender lady in them is wrong. There are small wheelchairs, but they do not have the same quality'. According to Ian, his new smart electric wheelchair designed as an office chair emphasises his masculinity more than before and in a much better way than his old chair had done.

Louise had altered her chair several times to perform her female needs better. She added a compartment on the side of her chair in order to keep a small make-up bag, keys and money. In addition she had the side guard rebuilt so that it could flip up and down, enabling her to move her body onto her bed, a chair, or the toilet seat on her own.

Both Henriette (45) and Lisa (24), being hard of hearing, want to change the representation of themselves on a day-to-day basis. They want to have the opportunity to change the colours of the earplugs during a day. One reason was to distinguish daily life from party life. Henriette says,

> I think there should be a choice for us grown-ups, and then I really mean grown-ups and teenagers as well. There should be more fancy things, in the same way as you wear a necklace, a ring or earrings or whatever. Why isn't it like that with hearing instruments? Like today, I would like a blue hearing instrument because I wear blue clothes.

Lisa's private audiologist was the first person who convinced her to try blue earplugs instead of flesh-coloured ones. Lisa was very confident with her audiologist and found her services very customer-oriented. This is quite different from

Henriette, who found her doctors were not customer-oriented. Lisa says (about her private audiologist),

> She knows me. She knows what I want, how I like it, what I want to get during a day, what sounds are good for me, what sound do I catch, what do I not catch. When I went to school, I could just pop in her office after school. Then they said to me, 'Can you wait for ten minutes or half an hour?' Or they said, 'It is a bit busy now. Can you come back tomorrow or the day after?'

She agreed with her audiologist to try the blue earplugs, because she had an idea that they might match her clothes. She said, 'I use many blue clothes, yes. So I thought why not try on a blue earplug'. In addition, she had her plugs decorated with nice looking stones. She received many positive comments on her new looks from family members, colleagues and friends. They asked her if the stones were real diamonds. But Lisa herself did not look upon her hearing instruments as jewelry. She said, 'It is definitely not jewels as I am total dependent upon it'. She had gotten tired of the blue ones and had tried to get another pair in another colour in order to distinguish between daily life and party life. She had not achieved this.

Henriette had for several years fought to get a white-coloured hearing instrument designed with several stars as diamonds. She was told by the service provider at the hospital that this was for children only. He had said that it was not a choice for adults. Henriette did not accept this and did not give in. After several years of fighting the system, she got the instrument she wanted. Tom (23) tells the same story. He had to fight to get a black-and-silver coloured pair, not because they were brand new on the market or because of their aesthetics, but simply because he could hear better with them. He also told me that he actually found them himself on the market and had more or less bypassed the hospital in order to get them.

Both Lisa and Henriette were annoyed with a wireless alert system that had been designed as a watch. Henriette's problem was that she was never given any information about the new alert system. When she learned about it, she applied for it, but did not get it. Lisa was upset because she found the watch unpractical. It was designed as a big, masculine black watch. This resulted in people taking off their own watches, using the alert system watch and forgetting their own watch. Her main question was why they had not designed the alarm system as a ladies watch too. After some time the company did so, but changed the design of it for women. For women it only resembled a watch, as a 'thing' to wear on the arm (not the wrist) by women. Lisa said that this was stigmatising: 'It has to do with appearance and design. It does something to you. Maybe you should be satisfied, but you are supposed to live with it every day. You get visitors, people coming and going in and out of your house. How do they think of you? It is the feeling of well-being'.

Conclusion

To date there has not been much sociological research on how disabled people think of design and aesthetics when it comes to AT. This chapter has revealed that these dimensions matter a great deal and that personal likes and dislikes with regard to aesthetics and looks might be a reason for abandonment. This is particularly the case if the user finds the AT product stigmatising.

Usability, including dimensions such as aesthetics and design, is important for well-being and quality of life. This has hitherto been a neglected issue in public service provision of AT. First and foremost, services emphasise utility and clinical needs. This chapter has discussed the perspectives of wheelchair users and people who are hard of hearing and put them as users in the 'consumption junction'. The user is at the centre of the network, and we have discussed the relationships among users, AT products and society. This has been analysed as a representation of different identities, as strategies of distinction and as different ways of opposing the patient role within the medical discourse.

Traditional ways of viewing and using AT within a medical discourse are put at stake by analysing how users talk about devices. This conveys different interpretations of AT, not as symbol of failure or personal tragedy, but as an enhancement and image and representation of oneself, such as age, lifestyle or gender. AT devices are thus important body parts, revealing one's personal identity. People alter, change and decorate devices, making them even more personal, such as adding a miniature silver skull decoration on the rim of the wheelchair or making a chamber inside the wheelchair for storing makeup, keys and money.

7 Integration of assistive technologies into domestic spheres and work life

This chapter focuses on the integration of AT into domestic spheres and workplaces. The aim is to grasp the nature of the relationships among user satisfaction, public service provision and the crucial role that devices play in people's daily lives. The process of acquiring AT is compared with the process of acquiring mainstream ICT technologies, as described by Silverstone, Hirsch and Morley (1994) through different phases: appropriation, objectification, incorporation and conversion (Ravneberg 2012). These phases are highly relevant for a comparative discussion on acquiring and integrating AT as compared to mainstream ICT.

One main reason for a comparison between the two types of technologies is that they both pose special problems to people. What they have in common is that they are not just objects to people. On the contrary, they are *communicative* objects. With regard to AT in particular, they are also very *personal* objects. These distinctions between AT and mainstream ICT on the one side and ordinary gadgets on the other side are, however, not absolute, but relative, as Silverstone argues with regard to ICT (Silverstone et al. 1994).

Safety alarms and signalling devices are examples of AT that act as communicative objects. Signalling devices alert, detect or warn; for example, they tell the user that it is time to get up, that there is smoke in the home, that there is a burglar or that someone is at the door or on the phone. They serve many different purposes and come in many different shapes and forms. Usually they are designed as boxes, lamps, clocks, watches, ornaments or jewelry. They can also be wireless. They have a central position in the home and are specially designed to attract attention from users by means of vibrating or blinking (Ravneberg 2012). Such functions distinguish both AT and ICT from other technologies (for instance, hair dryers, microwaves or printers). AT devices are also very *personal*, maybe more so than mainstream ICT devices. Users often perceive a wheelchair as more personal or closer to the person than a bike. Many users say that it is something you wear, like an article of clothing. Wheelchairs can be denoted as *rollwear* in this perspective and hearing aids as *hearwear* (Ravneberg 2009).

Chapter 1 argues that the design of AT devices can be analysed as gender scripts and/or as disability scripts. This is because AT devices tell stories about disabilities. Inscribed into the devices and the cultural integration process are different norms and values about disabilities. AT devices and their designs enable but also hinder or (dis)encourage activities, actions and mobility related to identity. In this chapter, we will take a closer look at devices as gender and disability scripts, by means of discussing their design, functionalities and the users' opinions about them. Do they represent a stigma one way or the other? How do the devices' design and users' opinions tell stories about contemporary society's views of age, gender and disability?

Appropriation phase – Revealing end-users as patients

What mainstream ICT and AT have in common is that they both provide important links between households/workplaces, individual members of households/work-places and the world beyond the front door. The recruitment of disabled people into the workforce often requires AT of some kind. AT is among the most important prerequisites for allowing the individual to do his or her work in the workplace. Based on interviews with disabled persons, we now turn to the acquiring process of AT, first and foremost in private homes, but also at workplaces. In the analysis, this process is compared with acquiring mainstream ICT devices.

The first phase as described by Silverstone et al. (1994) with regard to ICT devices is the 'appropriation phase', or the transaction process of the device, from being a commodity in the market to becoming an object. This phase is 'central to an individual's or a household's efforts at self-creation: defining and distinguishing themselves from, and allying themselves to each other' (Silverstone et al. 1994:1). The phase is described as a fairly smooth process for users of mainstream ICT devices. With regard to AT, however, it might take more time for the device to become an object for the person in question.

There are differences between workplaces and private households with regard to how long the process takes. Often the situation is that public AT-centres prioritise technologies to be installed at workplaces or at schools before private households. Tom put it like this,

> If I say that I need a new alert system at my office or on my phone or some-thing, I would send an application form together with my employer to the AT centre, and the centre would get it the following day. Then they might send a group of people to my office and two days after they will install it. If you need an induction loop at home or a blue tooth to your mobile phone, it takes a longer time.

Oliver states that he did not need to apply for any AT devices at his workplace. His employer had installed and paid for it before they moved to a new workplace, included the cafeteria. 'We have an induction loop in the cafeteria. We bought it when we moved in here. As simple as that, no ifs or buts'. Another impor-tant prerequisite for acquiring AT devices at work is to have a responsible and goal-oriented management. In Norway, since 2008 there has been a clear decrease in employment figures concerning participation of disabled people in the work force. Surveys show a reduction in the number of employees with disabilities during the last decade. From 2008 until 2012 the reduction was 4 percent, reduced from 45.3 percent to 41 percent. The figures are still low and considered disturbingly low compared to other countries (Wik and Tøssebro 2013). The Norwegian government implemented a job strategy for disabled persons in 2012 (in particular targeted towards young people under the age of 30), identifying four important barriers: *discrimination, costs, productivity and information and attitudes* (Norwegian Ministry of Labour 2012). The government emphasised that institutional cooperation efforts were needed between partners in the labour market (i.e., employers), interest organisations for disabled people (NGOs), the Norwegian Labour and Welfare Services (NAV), and other public services in order to ease the entrance into the labour market for disabled people.

One important factor that can facilitate the entrance of disabled people, besides reducing the above-mentioned barriers, is different types of emerging technologies.  Existing assistive technologies, such as accessible ICT or hearing and seeing aids, are becoming more advanced. New accessible ICT and web-based solutions have become important parts of this picture. Allocating, providing, adapting and maintaining employment support and AT to young disabled people requires the involvement of many different levels of service providers. The providers that most commonly are involved in this process are employment agencies, public AT centres and various centres of expertise, municipal health services, technical suppliers and local ICT consultants. All these different services are supposed to cooperate in testing, adjusting, implementing, maintaining and upgrading the AT in order to improve the work situation. The inclusion of disabled workers into the workforce is a challenge for work life. A management that sees invisible barriers and makes them visible is thus another condition that can reduce entrance barriers to the work force. The information on which this chapter is based emphasises that responsible management that can act on such barriers; however, often is *not* the case in many workplaces.

The appropriation phase of an AT device – when it is installed in the home – usually starts with the user searching on the Internet for more information. All the interviewees, and especially the men, presented themselves as very competent regarding how to use the technology they need. Their aim is to gather as much technical information as possible about the product before contacting the public service provider at the AT centre. The number of informants in this study is obviously too small to generalise, but it is clear that the men are very concerned with obtaining as much technical detail as possible. Oliver, an engineer with the greatest technical knowledge about sound equipment in particular, gave his assessment of the companies' websites regarding hearing aids. He said that there is very little technical information on their websites: 'If you look at the suppliers' websites, there is not much information to get. You don't find sampling rates nor possible technical details as you perhaps would have found elsewhere, if this had been some other kind of sound equipment'. When he asked some hearing agents why this was so, they did not provide a good answer. He said,

> One of the agents told me that it is available if you want it. The others said no, that this information will confuse more than it will help. The reason for this,

the agent explained, was that similar concepts could have different meanings and so there was room for different interpretations.

Oliver also observed that the information about the devices was divided among several pages on the websites: one page for 'ordinary users' (so-called end-users) and one for professionals. He describes the page for end-users as 'claptrap written with nice pics and so on. It is almost the same as you find in the brochures. Then there is another page for those who work professionally with it. There you find a little more specific information'.

The lack of access to information in the AT market, as Oliver describes it, can be compared to the medical market or the pharmacy market, where information traditionally has been provided for health staff. Our argument is that in the AT market hearing devices are largely treated in the same way as pharmacy products. End-users in the AT market can thus be seen as equivalent to 'patients'. For suppliers of AT, health staff might be the most important user group. Suppliers aim at developing a good interaction with the different types of users, but their primary target is health professionals. Suppliers are reluctant to give too many expectations to end-users, although there is pressure in the market to give more information to end-users, as one supplier in the hearing market explained in an interview,

When you're working in a health market where the products are paid for by the national insurance, it is the same as with medicines. You are careful to give users expectations about something they might not get. It is a balancing of the relationship to health staff. They are our actual customers. But then one finds out, like with medicines, that one could advertise products that didn't need a prescription. Then one had the opportunity to learn more about different types of medicine. There are books being produced on pharmacy where one can get some information about different products and expected side effects. So it is getting more and more focused on the user, that the user wants information.

By comparing AT with medical products, the supplier explains why the professionals are their actual users or customers. It is important to provide information without offending the professionals: 'It must be an interplay, because we don't want to offend the professionals. But they also understand that users want information. We are oriented as users today, and it will become more so in the future, that is for sure'. Thus, professional health-care providers have a lot of power in the AT market, similar to the pharmacy market.

End-users have less power or influence in this relationship. Patients becoming users has long been a major challenge for experts in health services, and this has been discussed for some years now (Alm Andreassen 2008). This structure in the AT market illustrates some important challenges or barriers with respect to user influence and user involvement in the appropriation phase of AT devices. As Oliver relates, it is hard for end-users to obtain technical information about devices. Information is targeted and differentiated according to different types of users. Service providers (professional users) get more specific and detailed technical information, whilst disabled persons, patients or end-users receive shallow information. The suppliers in the market adjust to this practice. Lack of first-hand information about technical details to ordinary users portrays disabled people as children or as passive receivers without enough qualifications to read, evaluate or interpret product information. Thus, it becomes a script devaluating disability. Consequently, disabled people cannot make decisions or choices on their own. As Oliver comments, 'The lack of information makes me feel stupid'. He has no influence on the choices made by producers, and he does not know what products are out there on the market.

The objectification phase – Decision-making processes on displaying devices, *or not*?

The next phase in the model of Silverstone et al. (1994) is the objectification phase, which refers to how users or members of a family express values, tastes and styles through the way they display the device at home, how they feel about it and thoughts they have about its appearance. This phase implies a clear focus on usability as well as aesthetics, as discussed in Chapter 6 (Berg 1994). According to Silverstone et al., the classificatory principles that inform the household's sense of itself and its place in the world are revealed during this phase, as they 'draw on perceptions of, and claims for, status and will express and in turn define differences of gender and age as these categories are constructed within each household culture' (Silverstone et al. 1994:22). This phase is also relevant to workplaces, because not all provided technologies turn out to be usable. Eva, for instance, has a mini induction loop on her office phone that is designed as a kind of necklace. In her view, it is not nice to look at, but it works: 'I put it on every time the phone rings. It is, of course, a bit extra work; it takes some time. First I need to wear it and then to put on the loop before I can answer the phone. But it works alright'. As discussed in Chapter 6, questions of aesthetics are important for users. Many express great dissatisfaction with their devices. Moreover, some do not install the device or do not use it in the house, due to lack of aesthetics. The dissatisfaction is also related to technicalities, as well as to how it fits with age, gender and lifestyle.

Inscribed into the devices and the cultural integration process are different norms and values about disability. Users regard some of the devices as stigmatising objects. From a disability perspective, this is a devaluation of disability. Oliver keeps his hearing instrument and a new alert system in the drawer. Neither fits him: 'Because I in some way did not think that the sound picture fit me. It makes me tired and I get a headache by using hearing instruments if the sound gets too sharp. When you hear ten times better than what you are supposed to do, it is not comfortable'. He also described a signal device, a bed vibrator, that vibrates too much and is impossible to regulate.

> It vibrated incredibly vigorously. It was quite extreme. It was connected to the telephone, to the fire alarm and to the doorbell. You could even connect it to the alarm clock. I did not have that. When I asked why it vibrates so

vigorously, they said that they had reckoned when they made the product that they wanted to make a product that catches as many people as possible, and senile people too, that have many other problems.

Oliver dislikes some devices that are standardised for all types of users. The vibrator was too energetic, he said, 'if somebody were at the door or if the fire alarm went off'. He did not need a vibrator that 'made the whole house shake'. He felt stigmatised by it. He laughed when he talked about it. Size was another reason for why he had not installed it: 'And then it has to do with the size of the box, it has to be that big, because when it shakes it produces too much heat and that kind of stuff. It has to be that big in order not to be flammable and burn . . . Yes, it lays nicely packed in a box (laughter)'. He is aware that there are alternative products on the market that could be better for him to use, such as wireless alerts. He just has not been able to get these items.

Lisa, a young girl also hard of hearing, is upset with a wireless alert system that had been designed as a watch. The watch enables her to walk from room to room without thinking of the need to see the signal. That was a good thing for her, but she soon found out that the watch was unsuitable for women, because it was designed as a big masculine black watch. Thus, it could be read as a gender script. An effect was that it resulted in women taking off their own watches and using the alert system watch instead, and forgetting their own watch: 'Then you end up walking around with a man's watch. It is very big'. She said that her interest organisation had contacted the manufacturer directly and informed them about this matter. This meeting between users and manufacturers occurred at a general assembly the year before. Lisa said, 'At the general assembly last year we contacted many producers. They came, took a stand and told us about the new technology. There were, of course, two or three who didn't show up. Then the question came again. Why was it not a ladies' watch, too?' The producer did develop a new device for women a few years later, but it was no longer a watch. It only resembled one. 'It is a dingus', Lisa said, laughing. The new device developed for women was to be fastened higher up on the arm where you never wear a watch. 'It is a kind of watch. It is smaller but it is not a watch. It is only a signal device now. It is smaller, designed for women'. Her question was why they had not designed the alert system as a ladies watch too, in the first place. She said, 'It has to do with appearances and design. It does something to you'.

Cultural norms and values about gender and disability are, as we see, inscribed into the technologies. The watch, the crystal polar bear design and different wireless alerts can be described as scripts, such as gender scripts or as disability scripts or both. It is supposed to help the individual to perform actions, but it can also be the other way around; it can limit actions or relations. For some, the watch is more helpful than the polar bear. For these users the watch supports action, not the polar bear. In the first place, the watch was designed for men. Then a new gadget came on the market designed for women. The new watch for women had one important flaw – it only resembled a watch. Thus read as a disability script, it became a stigma, devaluing disabled women in need of the alert system. Because the users do not want to use the device due to such stigmatising flaws, the technology limits the user's actions and relations. In a subtle way, these practices convey discriminating barriers in society towards disabled women who are hard of hearing.

Hanna was shocked to see how her new alert-system worked: 'Yes, it was really a shock. Many red lamps were installed. It looked like flashers on the car. It was red lamps, small triangles around the house. When somebody rings the doorbell or when the phone rings, it shines red all over the house. It is very nice, but it is like – look at me, I have a hearing problem'. She finds the alert system awful and stigmatising. 'It was very nice in the bathroom and down in the first floor/basement. There it worked very well. But in the living room I found it dreadful. Getting visitors and having the lamps begin to shine is terrible, even if they are small and discreet'. Later on, she got a new alert system that was integrated in a crystal polar bear that she found nice and aesthetic. The alert device was camouflaged in a crystal ornament for the house. The only drawback was that she had to carry the polar bear with her from room to room if she wanted to see the signal. She had wanted the same wireless system like the watch mentioned above, but she could not get it from the public service provider in the municipality where she lived.

The supplier of the above-mentioned watch explained that the watch was a little bit too expensive for the public AT centres. He added to this that it also had to do with attitudinal features at the AT centre: 'Different AT centres in Norway have different attitudes towards what they see as necessary for the user, and what they don't, and again, maybe they assess the user a little bit too'. Thus barriers of attitudes, as well as costs, prevail in the AT market, together with as we have seen, barriers of information and of discrimination. These barriers reveal what place and status disabled people have in the world. Thus, by not displaying or using some of the devices or expressing opposition to the practice, users voice their values, tastes and styles.

The incorporation phase – Renegotiations, replacements and non-use

In the incorporation phase, the focus is on aspects of the internal structure of the household or the workplace for that matter. This phase concerns how the devices are used and follows up on how the technology is being integrated into the routines of everyday life. This phase in the model of Silverman et al. (1994) is also different with regard to AT, as many of the AT users struggle with renegotiations and replacements of devices over long periods of time, rather than the incorporation of them into daily routines. The trying-out period might last for many years in private homes as compared to workplaces. Hanna's story can illustrate this a little bit better.

Earlier we discussed how Hanna struggled with her newly installed alert system. After this, she got another signalling system as a replacement for the red lamps. Instead of shining lamps in every room, Hanna got a blinking polar bear. One implication of this was that she had to carry it with her from room to room: 'Yes, when I'm going to the toilet, the bathroom and things like that I have to carry that polar bear with me. I must have it when I go to the kitchen, when I . . . (she laughs). Yes, it is terrible'. In contrast to the red lamps, she found the polar bear pretty nice and discreet, as it was disguised in a handsome ornament made of crystal glass. Even her friends found it likable. 'They walk towards it and say, "Oh my God, is it blinking?"' Her conclusion was that it was nice but inconvenient to use in the house.

Asked the question as to whether the old solution had been better after all, Hanna answered, 'Yes and no. They found out that the red lamps were not so nice. Now I have two lamps instead, one in the living room and the other one upstairs'. The lamps were a supplement to the polar bear. 'I have two living rooms. I have the polar bear in the main living room and a small, nice lamp in the other living room, and then I have one lamp in the sleeping room'. She said that this new system functioned better to some extent. The new lamp design was much better than the old one, as she had found that the red triangles lamps could serve as a signal to people outside her house whether she was home or not. She had been afraid that this could be misused as an invitation to burglary. She had also had the experience that people, especially kids on the street, when they realised that she had these red blinking lamps, they pressed the doorbell and then ran away, just for the fun of it. She said, 'Yes, oh yes, especially when it was quite new and the kids in the street realised this, they first pressed the doorbell and then they ran away. And I ran around like a mad, because I could not distinguish whether it was the doorbell or the telephone that rang, so it took some time'.

To the question of whether she had any other devices in her home at the time of the interview, she laughed and said that she had taken them all away. She didn't have the two lamps anymore.

> No, I have found out that when I am in the bedroom, it is for a reason. I want to sleep. So then, they can press the doorbell as much as they want to. And they can ring as much as they want on the phone. Then I am asleep. I did this to get more private life, I guess. I have the polar bear. It is really very cute, and then I have two children that can hear. They take the telephone and administer the phone calls.

The technologies are supposed to help the individual perform actions, but as we have seen in these stories, they end up as disability scripts, limiting actions and even relations. The incorporation phase with regard to AT thus illustrates that many devices are difficult to use and to integrate into the household's daily routines due to flaws that turn out to stigmatise the user and, as a result, limit actions and relations.

The conversion phase – Personal values and societal norms

The last phase, the conversion phase, deals with how the technology is adjusted to the values of the users by the users themselves, and their view of how society is or ought to be (Berg 1994). This phase differs from the others, as it does not follow in time, but deals with reflections on what the users think about the society and the technologies. These are meanings that define the relationship between users and the outside world.

> The boundary across which artefacts and meanings, texts and technologies, pass as the household defines and claims for itself and its members a status in the neighbourhood, work and peer groups in the wider society.
>
> (Berg 1994)

The interviewees conveyed their views on society and technology in different ways. First, in the appropriation phase, users meet company's webpages that have been differentiated between users and professionals, giving shallow information to users and more detailed information to professionals. The interviewees' main concern is that lack of technical information about devices on company's websites actually renders them as a passive patient. This is confirmed by the construction of the end-user concept in the AT market, a concept that can be seen as a synonymous to the 'patient', giving the professionals more power. Then, in the objectification phase, users are concerned about how devices do not fit into their life according to their lifestyle, gender or age. Some are embarrassed about design and devices' appearances, and they feel stigmatised by the devices, in particular those technologies that 'flash' their disability to the neighbourhood. Standardised products for all types of users, irrespective of diagnosis, age, gender or lifestyle, are also stigmatising. The blinking polar bear made of crystal that Hanna finds cute, is not so appealing to Oliver, a young man in his twenties. The integration process of the technologies and, in particular, the incorporation phase of it stretches out in time due to negotiations, renegotiations and replacements of devices. This limits actions and relations. The result is that users take risks, dismantle installations and abandon devices.

Conclusion

In sum, Silverstone et al.'s integrative framework on how to get and integrate mainstream ICT objects into private households or workplaces over time has been used in this chapter as a point of departure to discuss usability and user satisfaction with AT devices. The chapter has shown that the integration of AT devices, such as signalling devices in homes, is a much more delicate matter and a more complicated process compared to mainstream ICT objects. Using the Silverstone et al.'s model, we have found longer periods of negotiations, renegotiations, replacements, abandonments and non-use regarding AT objects as compared to mainstream ICT objects.

Technologically there are many similarities in the roles of mainstream ICT and AT devices in people's homes, but the potential normalising and stigmatising effect that are attached to some AT products with regard to age, gender and lifestyle, and the 'paternalistic' way the AT market and public services are governed and organised, make a big difference. Expressions of dissatisfaction with aesthetics and

the feeling of being stigmatised by the 'one size fits all' ideology lead to abandon-ment of devices, from young people in particular. The chapter has focussed on the technologies and analysed them as gender and/or disability scripts. Devices, when seen as disability scripts, by means of having a stigma attached to them and thus devaluing disability, end up in drawers and cupboards. Devices initially made for men are difficult for women to use, thus devaluing disabled women. The paradox is that technologies supposed to help the individual to perform actions have the opposite effect due to stigmatising flaws inscribed into the devices.

8 Public reforms, innovation and change of service orientations

In many welfare states, AT markets are construed as a special state–market mix created to increase fairness of and access to services for users. State institutions and public local service providers, in collaboration with private actors, mediate many of the relationships between the assistive device and the user (Rose and Blume 2003; Ravneberg 2009). Nevertheless, countries differ with regard to how this state-market mix is organised. In addition, actors, such as public or private providers, users and their families, often have different opinions about the devices' usability and utility (Scherer 2002; Ravneberg 2009). This chapter addresses principal questions regarding the relationship between different market actors, such as public and private providers, users and their families. There is ambivalence among the generosity and restrictiveness of the welfare state, the 'free play' of the market, and the user's legitimate or non-legitimate wishes and requests for (tailor-made) public services. The purpose of the chapter is to discuss these ambivalences and to point at tensions among the actors.

From different companies' websites, we learn that AT is smart, special, exclusive and difficult to obtain. AT makes everyday life easier for people and is supposed to prevent everything from bodily weariness to serious accidents at home. In general, AT is supposed to support people, young or old, in performing various practical tasks in daily life, at school, at home or at work. AT is different from other technologies or possessions that people might have. To users, AT devices do not have the same value as other possessions. In fact, they are much more contested (Scherer 2005; Pullin 2009; Watson 2002; Olaussen 2010). For obvious reasons, people are very dependent on AT. The concept *assistive* designates technologies designed for people who are or might be entitled to help from the public service system. In many West European countries the state chooses and usually pays for some or all of the technologies. In a country like Norway the state is the sole or major buyer of AT. This means that there is a larger distance between receivers of public AT services and producers, compared to mainstream technologies in a so-called free market. AT devices are normally more expensive and in some way disconnected from ordinary market structures. The distribution of products takes place in what we can call special 'hybrid' markets, consisting of state and private providers in various mixes. This market structure is more similar to the oligopoly market structure in which a few firms dominate. Consequently, this can lead to reduced competition among companies and thus to higher prices.

Theoretically, the chapter draws on Foucault's concept of governmentality, a concept that has been explicated as 'the conduct of conduct' (Dean 2007:47). This broad meaning of governmentality is used to describe how welfare states structure and govern a field, in this case, the service provision of AT. The structuring of a field produces choices for the participants, either limiting or extending possible conduct (Tremain 2005). Governmentality is influential within the wider society as well. It affects the thinking of people and limits or widens people's sense of social and political possibilities as well as their self-representations. Service orientation reflects governmentality, affecting and shaping in some way who and what the users are or should be. It works through the choices, desires, aspirations, needs and lifestyles of individuals and groups. It is a certain outlook on how to meet people. Deborah Stone (1984) argues that disability is not a clinical concept but a social and political category made by the welfare state. Thus, clinical priorities can be challenged by other priorities. We will take a closer look at such challenges in the following sections.

New public reforms inspired by the social model

The governmentality of AT in countries like Norway and England has some similarities in service provisions and orientation, but organisationally and structurally it has been very different. The medical model, applying a clinical design, has historically dominated the provision in both countries. This is different from a social model that applies an aesthetic or individual design (Sapey et al. 2004). According to the Health Department in England, the priority for each user has always been the clinical need rather than aesthetic appearances. However, critical voices after the millennium have pointed to the fact that to place AT within the health care system makes users passive, frustrated and bitter. They lose control, and their choices with regard to identity formation are limited (Ratzka 2003).

In light of this, and at a time when individual taste, choice and consumerism are more important than ever, one would expect that service orientations, user identities and governmental practices within AT would have changed. This is the case to some extent in that the link to medicine is not as obvious as it used to be. In some countries, services are becoming less 'medical' or patient-oriented, and more consumer-oriented, based on individual choices (Craddock 2002; Scherer 2002). In regard to products for children in particular, design has changed during the last decades, moving towards a more aesthetically pleasing, flexible, gendered and fresher, 'non-medical' appearance.

Since the new millennium, several European countries have initiated reforms in order to improve public AT services. These reforms have had a whole-systems approach in response to the negative effects of earlier new public management reforms in the public sector (Christensen and Lægreid 2007). The National Health Service in England recognised, for instance, that services had not taken all of the clients' needs into consideration (Department of Health 2006). The new goal was to obtain more usable, flexible, user-friendly or user-oriented systems by improving coordination as well as integrating services. The whole-of-government approach inspired new reforms in England, arguing for viewing wheelchair services as part of a whole-systems approach to independence. The idea was that services should be a coordinated system and experienced as such by users:

> A whole-systems approach is needed that encompasses not only posture and basic mobility but also the well-being, lifestyle choices and emotional and mental needs of individuals. This will require a change in service culture to one in which the social model of disability is seen as a fundamental value and provision promotes social inclusion and increased opportunities.
>
> (Department of Health 2006:6)

In 2007, the major goal for NHS services in this field in England was to improve access to audiology services (Department of Health 2006). In Norway, a similar thought inspired the reform called NAV, the Norwegian Labour and Welfare Organisation. On July 1, 2006, NAV was established as a comprehensive welfare reform targeted at all services for people in need of public support. The users' perspectives and needs were of major concern in the implementation of the reform. A clarification of needs and the correct use of means were important in securing inclusion into work life. Service, respect, information, access, competency and discretion were important values for the new NAV service. The social model of disability as described in Chapter 1 clearly inspired the recommendations in both England and Norway. The Department of Health in England pointed to the need for changing the system: 'Put the individual in the centre' and 'The system should work around me!' were some of the slogans behind NHS from 2006. The same individual approach was behind the NAV reform in Norway.

An historical comparison of the organisation of AT products in Norway and England

Traditionally, the Norwegian welfare state has been associated with a democratic welfare state model, in contrast to a more liberal model, such as that used in England, Australia or New Zealand (Esping-Andersen 1990). The Norwegian welfare state has some specific traits that distinguish it from the continental corporative or liberal models (Esping-Andersen 1990). The liberal model, which has been present in Great Britain, and even more so in Australia and the United States, is associated with extensive needs testing, a modest infusion of universalism, a weak state and a strong market economy (Helgøy, Ravneberg and Solvang 2003). In Norway, the welfare state model has been associated with universalism with regard to benefits and allowances, a stronger state and a more regulated market. Thus, in many countries the mixture of market and state provision differs for this service. In some countries the market is highly state regulated, as in Norway. In other countries, the market is less state regulated. Here private or philanthropic actors, as well as the state, participate as both buyers and sellers of AT, in addition to providing AT to users, as in England. In most countries, however, the provision of AT is state-generated.

The organisation of AT service provisions has changed several times since the 1980s in several countries. In Norway, the market has been centralised and state regulated, whilst in England it has become more decentralised, varied, privatised and less regulated. The major aim of the English reforms has been to obtain greater access to services, whilst the major aim behind the Norwegian reforms has been to obtain fairness of services. In order to improve services, new reforms were developed as previously mentioned, but these were criticised by organisations for the disabled for not considering all needs.

Thus, when it comes to the provision of AT in a country like Norway, one would expect this market to be strongly steered, and this is the case. In Norway, the provision has been and still is, national and hierarchical. It is organised as a centralised, state-regulated service provision. The Norwegian state is the sole buyer and 'user' of assistive devices. It has undergone three reorganisations since 1979. The establishment of the first assistive technology centre (ATC) in Norway in Telemark in 1979 represented an initial break with the medical model and a 'pure' clinical service orientation in Norway (Falkum 1984). Expert knowledge other than from the medical field gained access to service provisions, such as pedagogical and technical expert knowledge. This changed the knowledge base of the institution away from the 'pure' medical.

All types of long-term AT, except for hearing instruments, which are distributed by hospitals and private doctors, are distributed through the Norwegian county-level services. The municipalities distribute short-term AT, such as crutches, rollators, shower chairs, manual wheelchairs and AT for personal hygiene. Service technicians at the municipalities thus assemble, adjust, repair, transport and collect AT accordingly. The county services have an overarching, coordinating responsibility for assistive aids on a long-term basis in their county. To distribute AT in accordance with the NAV's rules is their administrative responsibility. Thus, the NAV has the overall professional, financial and administrative responsibility for assistive aids in the country. The NAV enters into framework agreements with individual and private suppliers. This constitutes a national assortment of good quality AT at an acceptable price. In other words, it keeps prices down. The ATCs in turn choose their local assortment from the national assortment. The ATCs also have their own maintenance service for their assorted devices. This contributes to a smaller choice for end-users, as there is a limit to what an ATC can repair without needing help from the company that produced it in the first place. It is the local health and home care services that have direct contact with users, not the ATC. Financial support is granted under the Norwegian National Insurance Scheme. The available devices have to be the most reasonably priced types of AT that meet the users' needs.

The national assortment system in Norway is different from similar public services in England, where the state might outsource the task to private companies. If the national assortment in Norway does not include any AT that meets the user's needs, the user *can* apply for dispensation to purchase other aids. The prices for such devices are negotiated, and they are then included in the national assortment. Furthermore, there must be a very good reason for making this application. In other words, the aesthetics of the device is not a good reason to get dispensation. To make it easier for users to get what they need as quickly as possible without going to Canossa (a humiliating system in which the user has to visit many offices and explain their problem again and again) or spending too much time waiting for their AT to be repaired, the NAV has introduced a so called user's passport. Users who hold a passport can contact vendors or the ATC directly to get the aid and the maintenance they need. This is practiced as long as the price has been negotiated and the device is included in the national assortment.

In England, service provision is more diverse. The state is not the sole buyer or user of AT, but the major one, and wheelchair services as well as audiology services can be provided privately. In England, voluntary organisations may also have particular expertise in dealing with AT (such as the Royal National Institute for Deaf People [RNID] or Red Cross). Let us take wheelchair services as an example. They have been privatised, decentralised and less regulated by the National Health Service since 1987. The McColl report (published in 1986) recommended restructuring wheelchair services to provide more accessible local services. Wheelchair services were transferred to the management of the Disablement Service Authority (DSA) between 1987 and 1991. The DSA was established for an interim period of three years and was then abolished in 1991. A further restructuring was conducted in 1991. This change represented a decentralisation of services, devolving to 151 local health authorities and self-governing NHS trusts. From 2001, wheelchairs were supplied by primary trusts. The system thus changed from being hierarchical and national to local networks. To allow people to purchase a wheelchair not provided for by the NHS, a voucher scheme was introduced in 1996. The aim of the voucher scheme was to give disabled people a greater choice of wheelchairs within the NHS. This is similar to the aforementioned user's pass in Norway, but with more options for the user. The system offered users three options: (i) accept the wheelchair prescribed, (ii) contribute to the costs of a more expensive wheelchair of their choice and be responsible for its maintenance and repair, or (iii) leave maintenance and repair to the NHS (Health Service Guidelines).

Decentralisation and privatisation have led to innovations and better services for users in England. In contrast to Norway, private companies in England have had greater direct contact with users, or so-called end-users (see Chapter 7 for a discussion on the concept of end-user). The system became more flexible and varied in England. However, decentralisation might lead to more inequality in state service provision among counties, making it important which county you live in. A centralised system, as in Norway, in which the state is the sole user or buyer of AT, might achieve more fairness in services throughout the country. On the other side, such centralisation can hamper flexibility and innovation because private companies, ATCs, producers or industrial designers do not have a direct link to end-users.

The marketing of devices and user's position

Many studies show that disabled people have been frustrated and unhappy with service provision of assistive technology in Norway, England and the United States (Helgøy et al. 2003; Sapey et al. 2004:68; Ravneberg 2009, 2012). Wheelchair design has made significant advancements since the 1990s. Much effort has brought attention to the person (Karp 1998). Hearing instruments have also gone through a technological revolution and have become digitised since the beginning of the 1990s. Despite this, when it comes to aesthetics and flexibility, the development of assistive technology institutions can be characterised as a slow evolution rather than a revolution. Despite the digital revolution in hearing technology, the market has seen a slow development with regard to design. Individual choices, expressions of dissatisfactions about aesthetics or conformist passive consumer attitudes are not reaching those who can move new designs off the drawing board. Small producers, eager to innovate, find it hard to survive in such a climate (Karp 1998). The pattern is that big companies swallow small producers, such as the German company Sopur, bought by Sunrise Medical in 1992, or Küschall, which became a part of Invacare.

Following Deborah Stone's (1984) argument that disability is a social and political category created by the welfare state, clinical priorities can be challenged, for instance, by demands for more aesthetically pleasing AT or more flexible AT/ICT. In light of the social model, this would be a valuable asset in order to integrate people into the community. One cannot take for granted that aesthetic appearances or flexible products necessarily contradict clinical priorities. Design deals with both function and appearances. It is thus worthwhile to study how aesthetics and flexibility are emphasised within the provision of AT, as this is very important to people. According to the social model, putting weight on aesthetics and flexibility would be one way of making devices more mundane, common and universal. Glasses and scooters are a good example of AT that have developed in such a direction. From an STS point of view, (so-called) end-users are intrinsically important for innovation (see Chapter 7 for a more thorough discussion of the term *end-user*). Users are the link to improve product design (Oudshoorn and Pinch 2003). In many AT markets, the link between designer/producer and end-user is, as already mentioned, weak. For designers, the users of the product are not only the end-users (that is the receiver of the service provision; the disabled person himself or herself), but the whole range of actors in the market, such as health personnel or other professionals. Traditionally, end-users have not participated in the design process from the beginning. The production process often develops according to the needs of a small selection of users. The challenge is that this selection might not be sufficiently representative. Historically, disabled people have established many companies, both in Europe (e.g., Küschall) and in the United States (e.g., Quickie) (Karp 1998). When disabled people themselves establish companies, this obviously strengthens the links between users and designers and contributes to better design.

Although changes towards better design of AT, such as wheelchairs and hearing instruments, have been implemented since the 1980s, the position of so-called end-users is still weak (see also Chapter 7). Expressions of dissatisfaction regarding the aesthetics from users have a long way to go before they reach producers and designers and eventually lead to innovation. Let us take a closer look at the marketing of hearing instruments and wheelchairs. Traditionally, hearing instruments have been marketed as a personal and invisible product. Producers' websites address those people in need of hearing aids. Compared to glasses, the marketing seldom relates to personal dimensions, that is, to the way you *look* (smart, fancy or modern) when wearing the instruments, as compared to advertisements for eyewear. The overall message from the marketing of hearing instruments in many countries is that they are 'noise on your personality', and consequently, hearing loss is something to hide.

Wheelchair advertisements are even more general. The text does not address you directly, but is geared towards users in general or to public service providers. It merely gives a description of the devices and of how well they function. The marketing is concerned with the functionality or utility of the device. An example is the possibility of bringing the wheelchair along in your car. The advertisements might state that the chair is attractive, but they do not elaborate on this. The attractiveness seems to lie in its functionality more than its aesthetics. Consider this example: 'The chair is good because it has a swingable and removable front section and can be stowed behind the driver's seat in a car'. Thus, wheelchairs are often marketed as an answer to a bodily shortcoming, as a physical problem in need of repair. Now consider an advertisement for glasses: 'Choose the style that appeals to you – buying glasses online!' The text addresses you, and only you, directly. It puts heavy weight on style, appeal, material, design, shape and colour.

Empowerment and consumerism

A shift in service orientation from patient to customer and a shift in governmentality in the AT market from utility to usability might contribute to facilitate societal processes directed at reconstituting disabled bodies as active agents and not as 'inferior bodies stripped of agencies' (Oliver 1990; Paterson and Hughes 2002). Such a reconstituting process is empowering. A consumerist approach would argue that expanding choices for active consumers of public services would enhance equality (Clarke, Smith and Vidler 2006). Through consumption and choice, such as consumer power, women and men are provided with important resources that can empower and enable them to become embodied feminine and masculine subjects. In this respect, consumerism might be a progressive challenge to producer domination and bureau-professional paternalism (Clarke et al. 2006).

This is not to say that greater consumerism solves all problems. We cannot take for granted that the interests of users coincide with the interest of producers (Newman and Vidler 2006). Consumerism also has limitations. If seen as a regressive individualisation narrowing collective democratic engagement, it will have limitations (Clarke et al. 2006; Clarke, Newman, Smith, Vidler and Westmarkland 2007). Consumer culture can be a site for identity politics, but it can also be a displacement or subordination of politics (Bauman 1998). If women's bodies continue to reflect patriarchal norms and aesthetic codes of 'femininity', rather than expressions of a self-determined individuality (Jagger 2002), the consumer approach might not be adequate.

The growth of a consumer culture and the conception of citizens as consumers seem to have had some impact on the Norwegian AT market. Reforms, such as the individual plan for access, represent a small step in this direction. These reforms are supposed to build services around the interests of the users, aligning with the whole-of-government approach. As sources of identity are increasingly derived from consumption and leisure rather than from work and production, (Jagger 2002), the use of AT is not an exception. The marketing of AT is a source for identity formation and strategies of distinctions that go beyond the discourse of the medical model. The disabled body is a key site for cultural intervention. Nevertheless, the ability of consumption to empower is important but must be balanced against the tendency of consumerism to reproduce inequality. This double-edged nature of consumption raises important questions regarding the role of the welfare state and the way public provision of AT should be institutionalised in the future. As Rose and Blume (2003) emphasise, potential users of technologies are not a homogenous group. They are heterogeneous, both as a collective group and as individuals. When products are unleashed by designers, artefacts become available for later reconfiguration as they are returned to the hands of human agents for more or less creative redefinition, re-evaluation and even re- (or de-) construction. Thus, artefacts represent different things to different people. Whereas some can abandon it to the junk heap, others can destroy it, while still others want to keep and even use it.

9 Universal design and assistive technologies

A challenging relationship

So far, the argument in this book is that AT is something more than mere compensation for functional limitations. AT also encompasses types of individual design representing personal identities and abilities. This perspective concurs with a 'design for me' approach. Individual design – or 'design for me' – is the user's own perspective: 'It is tailor made to fit the needs of the individual, where full personal control is seen as a prerequisite for high quality' (Anderberg 2006:51). However, talking about access, there is also a 'design for all' – or universal design (UD) – approach to be considered. Accessible public spaces and environments, free of obstacles, are important for disabled people, as well as for others. The challenge is that there exists no standard individual accessing public places and environments, but a multitude of individuals with different abilities, wishes and personal standards. This challenge is a topic discussed in this chapter.

The term *universal design* stems from the United States. In Europe, the term *design for all* is more common, whilst *inclusive design* is a term mostly used in Britain. In this chapter, we use the terms universal design and design for all more or less synonymously. Our understanding of UD is very much in line with the definition stated in the UN Convention on the Rights of Persons with Disabilities (CRPD) from 2008, a definition that is internationally accepted today. The UN convention not only connects UD and assistive technologies, it also provides a comprehensive understanding of equal rights for disabled people and raises awareness with regard to respect for the rights and dignity of disabled people. The convention is not based on either the medical or societal model of disability, but on a relational approach that sees disability as the result of an interaction between the individual and the social, cultural and physical environment (Lid 2014). As stated in article 2 the convention emphasises design, usability and integrated solutions for *all* people: '"Universal design" means the design of products, environments, programs and services to be usable by all people, to the greatest extent possible, without the need for adaptation or specialized design' (Lid 2014:18).

A common understanding of the relationship between universal design and assistive technologies is that universal design 'aspires to address the needs of the widest possible audience in the mainstream, whereas assistive technology attempts to meet the specific needs of individuals' (De Couvreur and Goossens 2011:108). One can say that AT more or less is synonymous with the 'design for me' approach and UD with the 'design for all' approach, but to draw the line between the two approaches is a complicated matter. The topic of the chapter is to address the relationship between the two approaches, 'design for me' and 'design for all', by the way of discussing the space between the individual and the (built) environment when it comes to design and the positioning of the technology within this space.

Universal design – An essential, disputed concept and a 'wicked' issue

It is difficult to give an exact definition of UD. It is a controversial and disputed concept in itself. Some authors define UD as an attitude; others state that UD is a utopia or a 'normative design domain' (Heylighen 2014:1361). Still others say that UD is a social movement, a voluntary philosophy, a process, a legal code or a result (Carr et al. 2013). Some claim that UD is a relational and contextual concept, a strategy or a value-based policy (Lid 2014). Others again say that the notion of *universal* should be substituted by that of *variation*, as UD actually deals with the inclusion of diversity (Winance 2014).

Both disability and UD involve a complex person–environment interplay (Lid 2014). By nature UD is 'a complex topic because it involves a concept of person, the environment and the interaction between the two' (Lid 2014:1343). This is also emphasised by Winance, who argues that it is 'important to analyse people's experiences in order to understand how their in/capacities come about and to understand the different facets of the interaction between people and the object or environment they use' (Winance 2014:1334). In order to establish a joint desired goal of standards, seven principles for UD were developed by the Center for Universal Design in North Carolina in the 1990s (Connell et al. 1997). Several authors state, however, that the principles have too much of a functional vision of use and the abilities of users (Bickenback 2014; Winance 2014).

In this chapter we are mostly concerned with the third principle: simple and intuitive use, meaning that use of the design is easy to understand, regardless of the user's experience, knowledge, language skills or current concentration level (Connell et al. 1997). However, we are also concerned with the first principle: equitable use, meaning that the design is useful and marketable to people with diverse abilities; and second principle: flexibility of use, meaning that the design accommodates a wide range of individual preferences and abilities.

Myriam Winance argues that the seven UD principles lead to a reductionist view of the user and of utilisation, because abilities are being ignored or disregarded. See, for instance, principle 3, where *regardless,* according to Winance, actually means without regard or consideration (Winance 2014:1333). As the designer must envisage a product that is to be employed by all users, the user is reduced from one with diverse abilities to a minimal user (Winance 2014). This might in our view be a matter of interpretation of the word 'regardless'. It can also be interpreted as independent of something, emphasising that UD is supposed to be easy to understand in the sense that it should be usable for all, irrespective of what impairments people might have. Thus, even though the principles behind UD are important and fairly well accepted by many planning actors and authorities as a desired goal in design, put into practice the principles are not without problems (Anderberg 2006:50).

UD represent a challenge to governments, designers and professionals. It is more or less impossible to be sensitive enough to all kinds of diversity. The designer, whether an architect or an engineer, has to think of and accommodate for a great number of personal solutions when it comes to UD. Diverging interests might obscure the potential for rational management and cost effectiveness with regard to UD. One example of this is Norwegian regulations that requires that at least 50 percent of all new buildings must utilise UD, even very small apartments (Construction's technical regulations, 2010 § 12-(1)). Building UD bathrooms is expensive, it is argued, and this regulation drives up building costs and, thus, excludes many people from buying their own home. Not all interests fit into schemes of reason or common sense, thus making UD a 'wicked issue' (Heylighen 2014:1365). However, Norwegian housing politics is different from many other European countries. It is for instance common that people own their own houses instead of renting them. Private actors and private building societies also have a greater influence on building processes and thus prices, rendering it difficult for the government to regulate the housing market. The private actors might argue that UD makes housing projects more expensive, thus making UD a complicated and expensive issue in Norway in particular. Others again, such as actors representing Norwegian disabled interest organisations or the government, might argue against this and claim that costs connected to UD are marginal (Lid 2013).

As we have noted earlier in this book, designers, producers and users are typically different persons, as Heylighen also states. An important implication of this is that the designer 'does not have direct access to the perspective of the ones s/he is designing for, rendering the designers involvement and empathy of major importance' (Heylighen 2014:1364). Thus, there is a great deal of power in the designer's direct experiences in shaping what they design. Nevertheless, as Heylighen states, 'the large majority of designers do not have any relevant personal experiences in being mobility impaired or blind' (Heylighen 2014). One example of how this might influence accessibility for blind people is closure of public transport's ticket offices and the introduction of ticket machines with touch screens at tram stations and such. Many actors have acknowledged that it might be impossible to design for absolutely everyone. In fact, many designers, architects, engineers and planners think that UD is a utopia, an attitude or a philosophy. Heylighen, however, questions this by asking whether the utopian character is inherent to the nature of design in general and not a characteristic specific to universal design? This question is reasonable to ask, according to Heylighen, as long as there is no direct and ultimate test of a solution to this 'wicked' problem.

Carr et al. (2013) argue that the built environment can create opportunities as well as constraints for elderly people to participate in social and productive activities. Universally designed spaces are according to Carr et al. more easily accessed and used by a spectrum of people without specialised adaptations. They emphasise that an advantage of UD is that it can provide accessibility without stigmatisation, by integrating accessibility features such that they benefit all users while going essentially unnoticed (Carr et al. 2013:2). This is an important and vital aspect of UD, which should not be neglected. The challenge, however, is whether or how this is possible to obtain for the variety of all users.

Information and communication technologies – design for all and design for me

Norwegian authorities point to full access and use of digital ICT for all citizens as a vital benchmark to full inclusion and societal participation of all citizens (White Paper, no. 17 (2006–2007)). One of the strategies applied to achieve this is to require all public bodies to implement universally designed ICT solutions, including hardware, software and interface, and to encourage all private agencies to do the same (Prp. to the Storting no. 44 (2007–2008); White Paper, no. 17 (2006–2007)). Web accessibility, however, is a multinational endeavor. Through the international Web Accessibility Initiative, Norwegian authorities participate in international efforts to establish joint guidelines for UD of ICT devices and user interfaces. The main point is that UD of ICT is the preferred and main solution for all. In cases where it is not possible to provide a main UD solution that secures access for all, accessibility for groups of citizens who cannot use the main solution shall be secured by allocating AT. A vital principle is that mainstream ICT shall always be compatible with associated AT. Whether or not this always is the case turns out to be another matter. Even though the widespread dissemination of ICT has provided disabled people new and enhanced opportunities in inclusion and participation, the digitisation of society has also created new barriers, such as an increasingly 'self-managing' society, which requires digital intuition, competence and literacy. This development represents challenges to digital inclusion for several groups of citizens.

For many people the widespread implementation of ICT in everyday life involves a dependency on accessible ICT at all times. For disabled people this very often also means a dependency on assistive ICT. The allocation of assistive ICT may lead to the anticipation that when assistive ICT is provided, access is achieved. Most assistive ICT, however, is reactive in design, and by the time accommodations are made mainstream, ICT has moved another step forward. If mainstream technology was universally designed, this time lag could be avoided. However, despite its benefits, UD is not a panacea for making ICT accessible for disabled people. The complexity of a digital environment and differences in how people access and use ICT may be beyond the reach of UD. Thus, the continuous development of usable assistive ICT is both necessary and complementary to UD, and it needs to be more innovative and proactive in its approach (Dobransky and Hargittai 2006; Emiliani 2006).

The mobile phone is one example of how a mainstream ICT, even though not universally designed, may replace the function of an individual AT, such as an alarm or a GPS. While the mobile phone represents a security net for many young people and their parents, this property of the mobile phone has had an even greater influence on young disabled people's everyday lives. The opportunity the mobile phone provides to call for assistance in cases of practical mishaps or when facing insurmountable barriers has increased and transformed many young disabled people's geographical range and independence in spatial mobility, and provided them access to places previously inaccessible to them (Söderström 2011). This use of a mainstream technology to secure individual needs is one example of how technological development and dissemination might close the gap between previously perceived ordinary and special technology.

An opposite example of this is assistive software programs, such as screen readers, for blind people. Young blind people like to engage in the same activities and conversations as their peers, and one popular activity and conversation topic is online videos, such as on YouTube. However, screen readers, which are intended to 'translate' digital interfaces, do not read websites with many graphics (Söderström 2009). The question is whether it is the AT that is inadequate or the adaptive interface that is not adjusted for screen readers. Is it possible to provide digital accessibility, in every respect, to everyone, at the same time? Moreover, who is responsible to ensure UD and equal accessibility in a global setting, such as the Internet, that includes both public and private parties?

The driving force behind the UD approach to ICT is welfare policy and an understanding of disability as a relational phenomenon (Lid 2014:25). Consequently, it is the adaptation and design of environments and society that is under scrutiny, through a UD approach. As we have seen, this approach sometimes needs to be accompanied by an AT approach. These two approaches exist side by side in official policies and documents, but they are rarely connected or confronted. This is not necessarily an antagonism, but it requires a deliberate consciousness about what approach to use in what context, and also how and why. A prerequisite to achieve this is to make explicit the reciprocal relationship between the two approaches. Instead of speaking with two tongues, one needs to bear two thoughts in mind simultaneously.

A continuum between universal solutions and targeted particularism

The topic of this chapter is not UD as a 'wicked issue', nor whether it is a utopia or an attitude. We are not trying to define the concept. Instead, we address the space between the individual and the built environment when it comes to design. In this discussion, we take into consideration UD as well as individual, tailor-made solutions. As we see it, this space is located along a horizontal continuum between universal (design for all) on the one side and targeted particularism (design for me) on the other. This continuum touches upon the dilemma of difference and sameness as discussed by Bickenbach (2013). The question he poses is what disabled people should stress, sameness or differences:

> Whether disabled people should stress their sameness with everyone else in order to obtain equality or stress their differences, in order to have the society

to respond to their unique needs and requirements, which if ignored would prevent them from effectively achieving political equity.

(Bickenbach 2013:1320)

Winance (2014) and Bickenbach (2013) argue that UD tends to ignore differ- ences. It pushes the separation between impairment and disability to the limit, or separates the body/subjective experience from the environment/policy, more or less ignoring the subjective. UD professionals might even retreat to a kind of professional paternalism, Bickenbach says. Winance argues along the same lines, that UD, by affirming the 'universal' as a guarantee of the inclusion of diversity, reduces diversity and ignores abilities.

In our perspective, disabled people need to fight for both equality (UD) and difference (AT) at the same time. In the space between the individual and the environment there are different technologies positioned, all with an aim to provide accessibility and usability for the individual. It is important to emphasise that such provisions, irrespective of whether they are universally designed or individual assistive technologies, do not stigmatise or discriminate.

The relational model and the complex person–environment interplay

It is important to underline that UD, or 'design for all', and individual design, or 'design for me', are largely complementary and compatible approaches with a common goal: the desired functioning of the individual. However, the two approaches do differ with regard to the positioning of the main technological solution. Whereas one technology is designed closely for the individual as a 'stand-alone' AT (that sometimes is mobile), the other is positioned in the surroundings as a more fixed or stationary 'stand-for-all' technology. As Anderberg (2006) states, AT implies a high degree of adaptation with the individual, thus emphasising that disability is to be seen as the product of an interaction between persons with impairments and attitudinal as well as environmental barriers, (the relational model that CRPD builds upon), different from the medical understanding of disability. The point is that a high degree of adaptation with the individual does not imply that adaptation with the environment is unwanted or unnecessary, quite the opposite:

> AT merely points to the fact that higher functioning control can be achieved in a system where assistance can be more personalized, and that assistive technology with high functioning power that follows the individual makes him/her more independent of the environmental changes.
>
> (Anderberg 2006:51)

Anderberg also states that design for me implies a higher level of participatory design efforts in which user involvement is important in the shaping of the whole support system. Inger Marie Lid (2014) argues that the knowledge UD builds upon is not only interdisciplinary but also transdisciplinary, involving user perspectives from outside academia. She asks for an interdisciplinary approach to UD that involves rehabilitation professions, such as occupational therapy, physiotherapy, social work, speech and language pathology and nursing; user organisations, such as disability activists; and planning professionals, such as architects, lawyers, economists, politicians and social policy makers. In our view, *both* UD and AT are interdisciplinary and transdisciplinary approaches.

Relying on individual technological solutions (AT) can be associated with the medical model of disability, thus portraying a negative disempowered image of disabled people. Our view is rather to the contrary. It is important to emphasise again that we do not see the problem as being with the individual (the medical model) and that design priorities should be individual solutions. We see the problem as being with the relation between the individual and the environment that hinders a person's right to activity, participation and citizenship. These questions also have an ethical character. We do not state that it is less important to build ramps and curb cuts rather than stair-climbing wheelchairs for the individual. The choice of positioning of the technology as 'design for me' (stair-climbing chair) or 'design for all' (ramps) is an ethical discussion on society level, as well as a question for the individual and the group. Lid (2013) states that UD conflicts can and should be discussed at all these three interpretative levels. At a macro (societal) level, UD relates to ethical questions, such as human rights and democratic values. At a meso (group) level, technical standards are tools for accessibility, interpreted and evaluated by the group. At a micro level, however, UD has a direct effect on people's lives and opportunities. This level has to do with usability, recognition, access and experiences seen from the position of the individual.

Possible dilemmas and incompatible considerations – Frictions in the city

An individually adapted wheelchair or a stair lift exemplifies 'design for me' technologies, whilst elevators or ramps often are presented as 'design for all' technologies. The relationship between these two positions is complicated, especially when it comes to choosing between the two different approaches. Lid (2014) states, 'The interaction between people and between people and the external environment is often characterised by friction to a greater or smaller extent' (p. 163). In cities, she says, frictions are unavoidable because so many different people have different plans and aims. The frictions have to do with both material and immaterial interactions, due to a lack of spaces in cities. Trams, buses, cars, cycles, businesses, cafes, pedestrians, beggars – all fight for the same space. The municipality, for instance, might build signage lines in a pedestrian area for people who are vision impaired. Then another office in the municipality rents the same street area to a private business that wants to establish a café or a beer garden there. Demand for UD increases frictions because the spaces in big cities are limited. Many things take place in small spaces.

However, big cities do work with UD. The city of Sydney can be an example here. On its website, we can read that Sydney has launched a comprehensive wayfinding and tactile signage network that will make the city more accessible for people of all abilities. The wayfinding system will

> link central Sydney streets using tactile and braille street signs, pedestrian-friendly maps, information pylons, new signs and digital technology . . . the completed tactile sign rollout will be the most comprehensive of its kind in the world. (http://www.visionaustralia.org/about-us/news-and-media/latest-news/news/2014/10/29/accessible-signs-open-up-sydney-streets-)

The wayfinding system is an example of how to make it easier for all to navigate. The Sydney city plan was in the first place meant for people who are blind or vision impaired, allowing them to navigate the streets with greater independence, ease and confidence. However, the aim was also to make street location information easier to access for everyone (Lid 2014).

A UD innovation like this is challenging and raises many questions. For instance, how will blind people be able to find the signs in the first place, and how do tactile signs make it easier for everyone? Another example is the mobile app Be My Eyes (www.bemyeyes.org). The application is supposed to connect blind people with volunteer helpers from around the world via live video chat. If a blind person is in need of help, they can receive it remotely through a live video connection, for instance if the blind person needs to know the expiry date on a bottle of milk or how to navigate new surroundings. This application raises many questions; for instance, how reliable is it, and what do you do when you are in places that have no Internet connection or if you are without a strong signal?

The work to make cities more accessible is not and will not be without frictions, and these frictions may not be the same for all. An important consideration must be to investigate more closely the frictions that occur in order to find for whom the UD solutions are not helpful or may even worsening the situation, and whose needs are not attended to at all. For example, not all people are able to walk very far and need transport. Another example of friction when it comes to UD and accessibility is that it might be necessary to have two stops on the same street for trams and buses due to UD demands for step-free access. Buses and trams have different heights and must therefore have different platforms in order to have step-free access. This issue can be seen as a matter of accessibility, but also as an element of UD. The point is, according to the UN convention, to give people equal rights for participation.

Other examples might be of a more ethical character. It is obvious, as Litvak and Enders (2001) state, that the more 'friendliness' that can be built into the environment, the fewer specialised supports the person will need to carry along. For example, having accessible buses reduces the hostility of the city environment. Litvak and Enders argue that if we continue to see these frictions as being with the individual, as opposed to seeing the environment or society as being disabling, the frictions might lead to design priorities for building stair-climbing wheelchairs (stand-for-me) rather than building ramps and curb cuts (stand-for-all). In some cases, stand-for-all solutions might eliminate the need for individual solutions, but it might also be the other way round: that individual solutions eliminate the need for stand-for-all solutions. Such frictions need to be investigated closely and analysed. The question is for whom the design is helpful and for whom it is not, and how to solve the problem in the best possible way. It is not always the case that UD, or stand-for-all solutions, are better or more preferable than stand-for-me solutions, or vice versa. On the other hand, solutions presented as universal (stand-for-all) but experienced as *not* (as stand-for-me solutions), might be conceived of as stigmatising technologies if they are not intended for the majority, but targeted towards a special group. If solutions only appear to be UD, they might offend people. Examples are some ramps or special entrances at the backs of buildings for wheelchair users. People feel they are being discriminated against when using devices such as ramps or wheelchair elevators at the backs of buildings, as these devices in a subtle way convey discriminating barriers in society.

However, stand-for-me and stand-for-all technologies might also be incompatible, as already pointed at. All people do not always require the same kind of solution. Curb cuts, ramps and accessible buses signal a welcoming attitude towards disabled people. On the other hand, it can be argued along with Winance and Anderberg that, in relying on the multitude of necessary adaptations of the environment, both manmade and in nature, disabled people lose control over where and when they want to go. The space between the individual and the environment is open for negotiations. An example can be in the cinema, if you cannot see what is on the screen. Then the question is whether to put on better glasses or make a request for bigger screens in the cinema? Another issue is audio-visual translation or subtitling for the deaf and hard-of-hearing at cinemas, which has been a fight for many years for people who are hard-of hearing. Should sporadic and occasionally made adaptions in places decided by others determine where people are allowed to go? In this perspective, it might be that in some situations individual solutions give more power to the individual.

Aesthetics and UD

UD can also be in conflict with aesthetic qualities. Aesthetic questions can be equally important as access, to be provided for by the governments, as Lid (2014) discusses. For instance, drawing from an example in Lid's book, a city decides to rehabilitate a big outdoor city space and builds stairs that lead down to a big lake in the middle of the space. The stairs are not secure, and the area beside the lake is not accessible to disabled people. It is thus questionable whether it is possible to make necessary changes according to the principles of UD as presented in the beginning of this chapter. The municipality of the city, however, claims that the stairs are part of the decoration of the place and as such are not part of the functioning of the place. The stairs are supposed to give the place a better look and aesthetic qualities. In addition, the stairs will give the place more varied and flexible use, because it is possible to sit on them or for children to play on them. Would UD require removing the stairs and replacing them with a slight ascent or curve instead, because not all people can walk the stairs, Lid asks (pp. 83–4)? Alternatively, maybe one could build both stairs and a slight ascent to safeguard both the decorative ambition and the accessibility to the area? Aesthetic qualities can be experienced through vision and through physical activities, while sitting or playing. The contrast or conflict is between human perception of aesthetic qualities and their valued symbols and the experience of not having access to part of an important city space.

Should all people be able to use the same area in the same way, or is it okay that access varies in a large city space? On the other hand, is this a question of discrimination against some people? Whose perspectives should have precedence in such a case? Is a stair or step 'reduced' to a barrier when it at the same time is an aesthetic decoration? If not, maybe one has to accept that not all have access to all of the space (Lid 2014:84).

This chapter has discussed different features and challenges of universal design and the relationship between universal design and assistive technologies. AT is more or less synonymous with the 'design for me' approach and UD with the 'design for all' approach. These two approaches are not always compatible for obvious reasons, and UD is presented as a 'wicked' issue. We have emphasised that to draw the line between these two approaches is a complicated matter. The relationship between them can be seen as a continuum – a line – from the universal to the individual (or vice versa) that needs to be negotiated in each case. We have presented dilemmas, challenges and frictions between AT and UD and within UD by way of discussing the space between the individual and the (built) environment and the positioning of the technology on this continuum.

10 Concluding thoughts for a multi-disciplinarian approach

AT + ca...d

In this book we have scrutinised the role of AT devices as well as the organisational structure of the AT market in relation to disabled people's lives. Technological devices are *actors* in peoples' lives. A main question has been how and why devices are a good match for people or not – in daily life, at school, at home or at work. AT devices are shaped to fit the wants and needs of those who can move them off the drawing board. In this process, the user might not be on board from the beginning or arrives late. An important question is thus to determine who has to be on board the boat in order to move it off. Organisational solutions that include the user's perspectives are vital. The participating agencies are often different mixtures of public and private service providers, suppliers, professionals (such as engineers, doctors, nurses or therapists), technicians, regulators, producers, designers, manufacturers, vendors and user representatives. Some of them have more power than others. Thus, the book also deals with the AT market and with participating actors and agencies working to match people and devices.

The book aims at providing a broader understanding of the multifaceted connections among disability, society and AT. We have done this by illuminating how all three elements are interrelated and mutual influential on disabled people's possibilities of action and participation. Our definition of AT is broad, defined as any item, piece of equipment or product which is applied to secure, increase, maintain or improve functional capabilities. AT devices are not intended for everybody but are targeted at disabled people and their functional capabilities. Over time, this has led to AT being loaded with collective cultural traditions, symbols and values, subjective feelings and meanings assigned to the technology. To illuminate how disabled people experience these traditions, symbols and values has been a central issue in our investigation throughout this book. This investigation has highlighted how different identity categories influence personal choices, experiences and reflections on AT devices. Usually, being disabled is not an important aspect of a person's identity or social position. Thus, disability is not the only identity category in focus.

In our effort to represent the voices of disabled people, we have drawn on different qualitative disability studies. In this book these are studies on elderly disabled people and AT devices at home, on disabled children's leisure activities and AT, on inclusive education and AT and on young disabled people's identity negotiations.

Furthermore, we discuss studies on the significance of AT design and aesthetics for adults, disabled adult's daily life and working life, UD, public AT services and the market.

Theoretical, practical and social implications of the book

Social and organisational implications

The ongoing, but slow process from a patient-oriented system to a more user- or customer-oriented AT system represents a challenge for services as well as for welfare states. In Norway the AT market is a national service with the welfare state as the *sole* buyer of AT. In England the welfare state is the *major* buyer of AT. The distribution of AT products takes place in what we have called a 'hybrid' market, consisting of state and private providers in various mixes. The market's organisational structure is similar to an oligopoly in which a few firms dominate. Consequently, reduced competition between companies and higher prices are challenges. In countries like Norway and to some extent England, the state regulates market prices, secures quality and gives loans of assistive devices to users. This structure has certain pros and cons for the user. It secures good, solid products at a reasonable price for the state, but deprives users of choice and control.

The discourse in the AT market is different from other markets. It reflects traditional ways of thinking within medical cure, treatment and rehabilitation. The AT market has many similarities to the pharmacy market. Most websites giving advice and information on medical prescriptions or AT devices address primarily health staff and service providers. Information for users is shallow. The term *end-user* denotes that there are several users in the AT market. For industrial designers the users might be those who deliver the AT device, maintenance technicians that screw on it, or people at the warehouse. Designers have to think about packaging, so that devices can be stacked on top of each other. For other actors, such as producers, suppliers or service providers, the users might be health staff, purchasers or the so-called end-users. For others again, the user is the welfare state. The term *end-user* reflects the last one in a row of different actors, agencies or users. The connection between end-users and designers/producers is a missing link in the structure of the AT market. One implication is that disabled people have less influence on design, such as usability and aesthetics. This market structure, combined with a clinical approach to disability within public services has construed a rigid service system. It disempower users of AT and reinforces professional power.

There is a need for communication among disabled people, AT producers, disability organisations and researchers. While universal design of mainstream technology is extraordinary important, it may not be enough. AT will always be assistive towards something that already exist. A major challenge is to make AT flexible enough to be innovative and proactive, and to carefully consider the technology's inherent symbolic values and their impact on the end-user. A priority in this field is to develop integrated services that really offer an integrated approach, such as greater flexibility and access to all necessary technology. This requires skilled and experienced professionals as well as up-to-date global searchable databases for equipment. This also means an integration of the total package of support in which all agencies are involved. There is a need for a structural change of the relationships among the state, markets and users to the benefit of the customers.

Practical implications

Although changes are taking place in AT services today, the book shows that such issues as the aesthetic side of design, identity and user satisfaction are important but neglected issues. A closer look at the multifaceted connections and interrelationships among AT, disability and society reveals that matching people and devices is not an easy task and that non-stigmatising, usable, well-designed, flexible and aesthetically pleasing AT is important for the people who are using it, whether children, adolescents, adults or elderly people.

Nevertheless, a service orientation putting less weight on clinical priorities has to some extent developed since the 1980s. There are some changes towards a consumer identity in this market, as opposed to a patient identity. However, this has been a slow evolution rather than a revolution in western welfare states. Many AT devices, however important, are by design disintegrated mundane life. They are either very clinically designed (e.g., chairs, alert devices) or targeted for a homogenous group of patients and come in 'one size fits all'. The AT devices might be helpful, but they are nevertheless special, clinical and not always good-looking.

Promoting participation in society is amongst the most important goals for AT devices. Let us take disabled children's use of AT devices as an example. Their use of AT promotes participation in physical leisure activities otherwise inaccessible to them. However, exploring how this technology might promote participation requires knowledge of the individual child's preferences as well as the diversity of technological possibilities. Most children and young people want to be able to choose their leisure activities by themselves, and want to have the possibility to choose between ordinary inclusive activities and special, adapted activities. In order for disabled children to have such a choice, it is not enough to provide a choice between ordinary and adapted leisure activities. Providing accessible transportation and premises, affordable activities and equipment, and social support and acknowledgement are just as important.

Practical situations and details reflect attitudes and competencies. In this book, we illustrate this by investigating everyday practices in mainstream classroom settings. While the socio-material practices of using AT in the classroom intend to facilitate the participation of disabled students, the inattentive moments of non-use of this technology place disabled students in social isolation. The constant shifting between use and non-use of AT characterises the socio-material practices of regular classroom activities in mainstream schools and is interpreted as an expression of a deficit-perspective of disability, and a subsequent individualisation of disabled students' education. Small technical errors and deficiencies, incompatible technologies, and the permeability of the material world and the digital world create digital differentiation, especially in the youth community. As long as universal design is not a reality, and AT lags behind mainstream technology, disabled people will feel they are being discriminated against when using assistive ICT or devices such as ramps or segregated wheelchair elevators. These devices are examples of technologies that are the opposite of universal design as discussed in Chapter 9. They put impairment on the centre stage and reproduce stereotypes of disability; thus, in a subtle way, they create discriminating barriers in society.

Integration of AT devices into homes, such as signalling devices, is also a much more delicate matter than integrating mainstream ICT devices and a much more complicated process for disabled people, with longer periods of negotiations, renegotiations, replacements, abandonments and non-use for AT objects as compared to mainstream ICT objects.

On the other side, installing new technologies into private homes for elderly people might improve their quality of life and contribute to helping them age in place in their 'sacred' homes instead of moving to an institution. Important issues for elderly people are the positive effects of AT devices on their independence, their participation in social life and their state of happiness with being able to stay longer in their own home. In the long term, AT devices also can reduce the amount of formal care spent on elderly residents in institutions.

Theoretical implications

The book has illustrated how a combination of STS studies and disability studies perspectives facilitates an analysis of the connections and interrelationships among disability, society, AT devices, markets, services and user satisfaction. In an STS perspective, technical devices have been fruitfully analysed as actors in themselves. This has facilitated a sharpened focus on the crucial role of AT alongside human aid. AT devices are not neutral to people in need of them. This important fact has to be taken into account in research on AT. More precisely, AT products, while seen as non-human actors, are more or less *social constructions* partaking in negotiation processes. An important question is how action for children, students, adults and elderly people is made possible or not possible by the way of technology.

By positioning the disabled person at the centre of the 'consumption junction' – in the crossroad of the network of actors and agencies – the network is viewed from the inside out, from the user's perspective. The main empirical focus throughout the book has been different mixtures of social (human) and non-social (technical) elements that participate in negotiation processes for people at all ages. We have termed our approach 'disability heterogeneous constructivism' (see Chapter 1) where the focus is on how technology – through its utility and usability – shapes and constitutes new forms of social relationships for the subjective person in question.

Both AT devices and people tell stories about contemporary society's views of disability. One reason is that designers of AT devices never work in a black box. They always try to anticipate preferences, motives, tastes and skills of potential users of the technology and the cultural norms in the society. Inscribed into

AT devices and the integration process of devices are different norms and values about, for instance, age, gender and disability. This is why analytical tools like gender and disability scripts highlight how traditions, symbols, norms and values are inscribed into devices. This perspective on disability and technology adds to our understanding of how AT devices both hinder and encourage activities, actions and mobility. The book thus connects technology and gender, seeing technology and gender as social constructs or as integrated social processes. Norms about gender, just like norms about age or (dis)ability, are built into devices and artefacts, without people reflecting so much about it in everyday life. Producers that make new innovative products inscribe a special view of the world and its users in the technology.

A gender script perspective states that devices always have reflections about gender built into them. Indeed, the technologies that surround us, such as alarms, hearing devices or wheelchairs, tell lot about norms and values with regard to gender in the society in which they are made. We have discussed such AT as alarm devices and analysed them as gender scripts as well as disability scripts. Devices speak an implicit language that says something about what producers had in mind when they planned and produced new technologies, and it tells something about anticipated needs. Gender scripts depict representations of masculinities and femininities in technological artefacts. Technology can invite or inhibit specific performances of identities, such as gendered identities and relations. Thus, it is no surprise that the integration of AT devices into homes, schools or workplaces is a delicate matter and a complicated process.

Although changes towards better design of AT have been implemented since the 1980s, and many of these changes have encouraged actions and activities for disabled people in many ways, the user is still positioned at the margin. To date, there has not been much sociological research on how disabled people think of the design and aesthetics of AT devices, but some studies reveal that design and aesthetics matter a lot and that personal dislike of the look of the AT devices might be a reason for abandonment or non-use. Design of AT devices not only deals with utility and functionality, but also with usability and human communication. Using AT objects is intrinsically symbolic, culturally and historically contextualised. As the book shows, neglect of aesthetics and design impedes on the creation of individualised feminine and masculine selves, as well as on identity negotiations. Using AT is more than overcoming environmental barriers. It is a form of communication and a representation of identities and strategies of distinctions. AT devices are part of the negotiation of identities.

Multi-disciplinarian research studies are needed on usability, interface, UD and the organisational structure of the market with all its agencies and actors/users, as well as on how devices function in society as identity markers. An important aspect of this research is how to reduce individual risks and losses as well as societal costs with regard to the use of AT.

The use and significance of AT have become a social phenomenon and should be studied in social contexts, just like age, gender or (dis)ability. One of the challenges we face is that if technology is to promote social interaction and participation of disabled people, we must recognise that disability and ability are not a dichotomy. People are enabled or disabled in many different ways and in different situations. Instead of pursuing an exclusive focus on AT as compensating technologies, we need to develop inclusive technologies which create room and acceptance for diversity and differences. The question is not how AT and advanced technological solutions may normalise human functions and actions. Rather, the question is how technology may create effects that help change the way we think about – and distinguish between – able and disabled and thus facilitate greater inclusion and appreciation of human diversity and differences.

Bibliography

Akrich, M. (1992) "The description of technical objects" in W. Bijker and John Law (eds.) *Shaping technology/building society: Studies in sociotechnical change*, pp. 205–244. Cambridge: MIT press.

Alm Andreassen, T. (2008) *Når pasienter blir brukere: en utfordring for ekspertisens posisjon i helsepolitikken* (in English: *When patients become users: A challenge for the position of the expertise in the health policy*). Oslo: Unipub.

Anderberg, P. (2006) *FACE. Disabled people, technology and internet*. Doctoral thesis, no. 1:2006, Certec, Division of Rehabilitation Engineering Research, Dept. of Design Sciences, Lund University.

Arthanat, S., Bauer, S. M., Lenker, J. A., Nochajski, S. M. and Wu, Y. W. B. (2007) "Conceptualization and measurement of assistive technology usability." *Disability & Rehabilitation: Assistive Technology* 2(4): 235–248.

Asbjørnslett, M. (2015) *"Ordinary kids" – Everyday life experiences of children with disabilities*. PhD dissertation, The Norwegian School of Sport Science

Asbjørnslett, M., Helseth, S. and Engelsrud, G. (2014) "Being an ordinary kid – Demands of everyday life when labelled with disability." *Scandinavian Journal of Disability Research* 16(4): 364–376. http://dx.doi.org/10.1080/15017419.2013.787368

Bailey, J. (1998) "Inclusion through categorisation" in R. Booth and M. Ainscow (eds.) *From them to us: An international study of inclusion in education*, pp. 171–185. London: Routledge.

Bauman, Z. (1998) *Work, consumerism and the new poor*. Buckingham: Open University Press.

Bedell, G., Coster, W., Law, M., Liljenquist, K., Kao, Y.-C., Teplicky, R. and Khetani, M. A. (2013) "Community participation, supports and barriers of school-age children with and without disabilities." *Archives of Physical Medicine and Rehabilitation* 94: 315–323. doi:10.1016/j.apmr1012.09.024

Bekken, W. (2009) *Foreldres erfaringer fra samarbeid og tilrettelegging for barn med synshemminger i skole En kvalitativ undersøkelse* (in English: *Parents experiences with collaboration for visually impaired children*). Oslo: Assistanse.

Bekken, W. (2014) "I want them to see that I feel normal: Three children's experiences from attending consultations in pediatric rehabilitation." *Disability & Society* 29(5): 778–791. http://dx.doi.org/10.1080/09687599.2013.874329

Berg, A.-J. (1994) "Technological flexibility: Bringing gender into technology" in E. Cockburn and R. F. Dilic (eds.) *Bringing technology home: Gender and technology in a changing Europe*, pp. 4–111. Buckingham: Open University Press.

Berge T., Øien H. and Jakobsson, N. (2014) *Formell og uformell omsorg: Samspillet mellom familien og velferdsstaten* (in English: *Formal and informal care: The interplay between the family and the welfare state*). Notat 3/14. Oslo: NOVA.

Bickenbach, J. (2014) "Universal design social policy: when disability disappears." *Disability & Rehabilitation* 36 (16): 1320–1327.

Blume, S. (1999) "Histories of cochlear implantation." *Social Science and Medicine* 49: 1257–1268.

Blume, S., Galis, V. and Pineda, V., (2014) "Introduction, STS and disability." *Science Technology & Human Values* 39(1): 98–104.

Bø, I. and Schiefloe, P. M. (2007) *Sosiale landskap og sosial kapital Innføring i nettverkstenkning* (in English: *Social landscape and social capital introduction to networking*). Oslo: Universitetsforlaget.

Boer, A., Pijl, S. J. and Minnaert, A. (April 2011) "Regular primary school teachers' attitudes towards inclusive education: A review of the literature." *International Journal of Inclusive Education* 15(3): 331–353.

Borg, J., Larsson, S. and Östergren, P. O. (2011) "The right to assistive technology, for whom, for what and by whom?" *Disability and Society* 26(2).

Bossaert, G., Colpin, H., Pijl, S. J. and Petry, K. (2013) "Truly included? A literature study focusing on the social dimension of inclusion in education." *International Journal of Inclusive Education* 17(1): 60–79.

Boström, G. (2008) *Hälsa på lika villkor? Hälsa och livsvillkor bland personer med funktionsnedsättning* (In English: *Health on equal conditions? Health and living conditions among disabled people*). Östersund: Statens Folkhälsoinstitut.

Breivik, J.-K. (2005) *Deaf identities in the making*. Washington, DC: Gallaudet University Press.

Browne, I. and Misra, J. (2003) "The intersection of gender and race in the labor market." *Annual Review Sociology* 29: 487–513.

Buckingham, D. (2006) "Children and new media" in L. A. Lievrouw and S. Livingstone (eds.) *The handbook of new media updated student edition*, pp. 75–91. London: SAGE.

Burnett, G. & Jaeger, P. R. (2008). "Small worlds, lifeworlds, and information: the ramifications of the information behaviour of social groups in public policy and the public sphere" *Information Research*, **13**(2) paper 346. Available at http://InformationR.net/ir/13-2/paper346.html.

Byrne, B. (2013) "Hidden contradictions and conditionality: Conceptualisations of inclusive education in international human rights law." *Disability & Society* 28(2): 232–244.

Carr, K., Weir, P. L., Azar, D. and Azar, N. R. (2013) "Universal design, a step towards successful ageing." *Journal of Ageing Research* 2013: 1–8.

Chatman, E. A. (1999) "A theory of life in the round." *Journal of the American Society for Information Science* 50(3): 207–217.

Christensen, T. and Lægreid, P. "The whole-of government approach to public sector reform." *Public Administration Review* 67(6): 1059–1066.

Clarke, J., Newman, J., Smith, N., Vidler, E. and Westmarkland, L. (2007) *Creating citizen-consumers: Changing publics and changing public services*. London: Sage Publications.

Clarke, J., Smith, N. and Vidler, E. (2006) "Consumerism and the reform of public services: Inequalities and instabilities." *Social Policy Review* 17: 167–182.

Connell, B. R. et al. (1997) *The principles of universal design*. Version 2.0–4/1/97. Retrieved August 17th 2016 from http://www.disabilitymonitor-see.org/documents/dmi2eng/annex2pdf

Cook, L. H. and Shinew, K. J. (2014) "Leisure, work and disability coping: 'I mean, you always need that 'in' GROUP.'" *Leisure Science* 36: 420–438.

Coster, W. and Khetani, M. A. (2008) "Measuring participation of children with disabilities: Issues and challenges." *Disability and Rehabilitation* 30(8): 639–648.

Cowan, R. S. (2012) "The consumption junction: A proposal for research strategies in the sociology of technology" in W. Bijker, E. Hughes, P. Thomas and T. Pinch (eds.) *Social construction of technological systems: New directions in the sociology and history of technology*, pp. 253–270. Cambridge: MIT Press.

Craddock, G. (2002) "Partnership and assistive technology in Ireland" in M. Scherer (ed.) *Matching device and consumer for successful rehabilitation*, pp. 253–270. Washington, DC: American Psychological Association.

Craddock, G. (2006) "The AT continuum in education: Novice to power user." *Disability and Rehabilitation: Assistive Technology* 1(1–2): 17–27.

Csikszentmihalyi, M. (1997) *Finding flow: The psychology of engagement with everyday life*. New York: Basic Books.

Cummings, J. N., Kiesler, S. B. and Sproull, L. (2002) "Beyond hearing: Where real-world and online support meet." *Group Dynamics: Theory, Research, and Practice* 6(1): 78–88.

Dean, M. (2007) *Governing societies*. Berkshire: Open University Press.

De Couvreur, L. and Goossens, R. (2011) "Design for (every)one: Co-creation as a bridge between universal design and rehabilitation engineering." *CoDesign* 7(2): 107–121.

Department of Health (2006) *Out and about: Wheelchairs as part of a whole-systems approach to independence*. London: Care Service Improvement Partnership.

Devik, S. A. and Hellzen, O. (2012) *Velferdsteknologi og hjemmeboende eldre. Hvilke gevinster er oppnådd med velferdsteknologi som kommunikasjonsstøtte for hjemmeboende eldre i kommunehelsetjenesten? – Og hva kan påvirke utbyttet? En systematisk litteraturstudie* (in English: *Welfare technology and elderly people living at home. What is achieved with welfare technology as communication aid for elderly living at home and receiving municipal care? A systematic literature review*). Report 79. Steinkjer: HiNT

Dobransky, K. and Hargittai, E. (2006) "The disability divide in internet access and use." *Information, Communication and Society* 9(3): 313–334.

Dugstad, J., Nilsen, E. R., Gullslett, M. K., Eide, T. and Eide, H. (2015) *Implementering av velferdsteknologi i helse- og omsorgstjenester. Opplæringsbehov og utforming av nye tjenester – en sluttrapport.* (in English: *Implementation of welfare technology in health and social care services. Educational needs and design of new services*). Series 13. Drammen: Høgskolen i Buskerud og Vestfold.

Education Act (1997) *Om lov om grunnskolen og den videregående opplæringa* (in English: *About act on the compulsory school and the high school*). Oslo: Ministry of education and research.

Emiliani, P. L. (2006) "Assistive Technology (AT) versus Mainstream Technology (MST): The research perspective." *Technology and Disability* 18: 19–29.

Engel-Yeger, B., Jarus, T., Anaby, D. and Law, M. (2009) "Differences in patterns of participation between youths with cerebral palsy and typically developing peers." *The American Journal of Occupational Therapy* 63(1): 96–104.

e-Norway (2009) *The digital leap*. Oslo: Ministry of Modernisation.

Erikson, L., Welander, J. and Granlund, M. (2007) "Participation in everyday school activities for children with and without disabilities." *Journal of Developmental and Physical Disabilities* 19: 485–502.

Ervik, R. and Lindén, T. S. (eds.). (2013) *The making of ageing policy: Theory and practice in Europe*. Cheltenham: Edward Elgar Publishing.

Esping-Andersen, G. (1990) *The three worlds of welfare capitalism*. Cambridge: Polity Press.

Falkum, E. (1984) *Hjelpemiddelmarkedets organisasjon* (in English: *The organization of the assistive technology market*). Dept. of Administration and Organization Theory, University of Bergen.

Froestad, J. and Ravneberg, B. (June 2006) "Education policy, the Norwegian unitary school and the social construction of disability." *Scandinavian Journal of History* 31(2): 119–143.

Gable, A. S. (2013) "Disability theorizing and real-world educational practice: A framework for understanding." *Disability & Society* 24: 73–80. doi:10.1080/09687599.2013. 776485

Galis, V. (2011) "Enacting disability: How can science and technology inform disability studies?" *Disability & Society* 26: 825–838.

Gamble, M. J., Dowler, D. L. and Orslene, L. E. (2006) "Assistive technology: Choosing the right tool for the right job." *Journal of Vocational Rehabilitation* 24: 73–80.

Garland-Thomson, R. (1997) *Extraordinary bodies: Figuring physical disability in American culture and literature*. New York: Columbia University Press.

Gieryn, T. (2002) "What buildings do." *Theory and Society* 31: 35–74. Kluwer Academics Publishers, the Netherlands.

Gjessing, B. (2014) *Mulig for meg! Barns erfaringer med aktivitetshjelpemidler* (in English: *Childrens experiences with assistive activity technologies*). Master thesis, University of Bergen.

Goffman, E. (1963) *Stigma: Notes on the management of spoiled identity*. London: Penguin.

Gulbrandsen, L. M., Seim, S. and Østensjø, S. (2015) "Teoretiske perspektiver og begreper" (in English: Theoretical perspectives and terms) in B. Fallang, B. C. R. Olsen, K. Opsahl, S. Seim, O. S. Ulvik, I. Øien and S. Østensjø (eds.) *Barns deltakels i hverdagsliv og profesjonell praksis – en utforrkende tilnærming* (in English: *Childrens participation in everyday life and profesional practice – An explorative approach*), pp. 37–55. Oslo: Universitetsforlaget.

Gulløv, E. and Højlund, S. (2003) *Feltarbejde blant børn: metodologi og etik i etnografisk børneforskning* (in English: *Fieldwork among children: Methodology and ethics in ethnographic children research*). Copenhagen: Gyldendal.

Gustavsson, A., Tøssebro, J. and Traustadòttir, R. (2005) "Introduction: Approaches and perspectives in nordic disability research" in A. Gustavsson, J. Sandvin, R. Traustadòttir and J. Tøssebro (eds.) *Resistance, reflection and change nordic disability research*, pp. 23–44. Lund: Studentlitteratur.

Habermas, J. (1989) *The structural transformations of the public sphere: An inquiry into a category of bourgeois society*. Cambridge: MIT press.

Haraway, D. (1991) "A cyborg manifesto: Science, technology and socialist-feminism in the late twentieth century" in *Simians, cyborgs and women: The reinvention of nature*, pp. 149–181. New York: Routledge.

Helgøy, I., Ravneberg, B. and Solvang, P. (June 2003) "Service provision for an independent life." *Disability & Society* 18(4): 471–487.

Helsper, E. J. (2011) *The emergence of a digital underclass. Digital policies in the UK and evidence for inclusion*. LSE Media Policy Project, Media Policy Brief 3.

Hemmingsson, H., Lidström, H. and Nygård, L. (2009) "Use of assistive technology devices in mainstream schools: Students' perspective." *The American Journal of Occupational Therapy* 63(4): 463–472.

Hess, D. (1997) *Science studies: An advanced introduction.* New York: New York University Press. Retreived from internet August 29th 2016 from http://www.vissionaustralia. org/about-us/news-and-media/latestnews/news/2014/10/29/accessible-signs-open-up-sydeny-streets-. Retrieved from internet August 29th 2016 from http://www.bemyeyes. org/press/

Heylighen, A. (2014) "About the nature of design in universal design." *Rehabilitation & Disability* 36(16): 1360–1368.

Huang, I.-C., Sugden, D. and Beveridge, S. (2009) "Children's perceptions of their use of assistive devices in home and school settings." *Disability and Rehabilitation: Assistive Technology* 4(2): 95–105.

Hughes, B., Russell, R. and Paterson, K. (2005) "Nothing to be had off the peg: Consumption, identity and the immobilization of young disabled people." *Disability & Society* 20(1): 3–17.

ICF-CY. (2007) *International Classification of Functioning, Disability and Health. Children & Youth Version.* Geneva: WHO.

Imms, C. (2008) "Children with cerebral palsy participate: A review of the literature." *Disability and Rehabilitation* 30(24): 1867–1884.

Imms, C., Reilly, S. and Dodd, K. (2008) "Diversity of participation in children with cerebral palsy." *Developmental Medicine & Child Neurology* 50(5): 363–369.

Ingebrigtsen, J. E. and Aspvik, N. P. (2010) *Barns idrettsdeltakelse i Norge – Litteraturstudie av barn i idretten* (in English: *Children's participation in sports in Norway – Literaturestudy of children in sports*). Trondheim: NTNU Samfunnsforskning AS senter for idrettsforskning Report 02/2010.

Islam M. K. and Ravneberg, B. (2009) *Economic effects of the municipality occupational therapy services in Norway.* Report 5:2009. Bergen: Stein Rokkan Centre for Social Studies.

Jaeger, P. T. (2012) *Disability and the internet confronting a digital divide.* Boulder, CO: Lynne Rienner Publisher.

Jagger, Elizabeth (2002) "Consumer bodies" in P. Hancock, B. Hughes, E. Jagger, K. Paterson, R. Russell, E. Tulle-Winton and M. Tyler (eds.) *The body, culture and society: An introduction.* Buckingham: Open University Press.

James, A., Jenks, C. and Prout, A. (2004) *Theorizing childhood.* Cambridge, UK: Polity Press.

Jokela, T., Livari, N., Maetro, J. and Karukka, M. (2003) *The standard of user-centered design and the standard definition of usability: Analyzing ISO 13407 against ISO 9241–11. Proceedings of the Latin American conference on Human-Computer interaction,* pp. 53–60. New York: ACM.

Kaare, B. H., Brantzæg, P. B., Heim, J. and Endestad, T. (2007) "In the borderline between family orientation and peer culture: The use of communication technologies among Norwegian tweens." *New Media & Society* 9(4): 603–624.

Kalyvas, V. and Reis, G. (2003) "Sport adaptation, participation, and enjoyment of students with and without physical disabilities." *Adapted Physical Activity Quarterly* 20: 182–199.

Karp, G. (1998) *Choosing a wheelchair: A guide for optimal independence.* Sebastopol: O'Reilly & Ass.

Kent, B. and Smith, S. (2006) "They only see it when the sun shines in my ears: Exploring perceptions of adolescent hearing aid users." *Journal of Deaf Studies and Deaf Education* 11(4): 461–476.

Kermit, P., Tharaldsteen, A. M., Haugen, G. M. D. and Wendelborg, C. (2014) "*En av flokken? Inkludering og ungdom med sansetap – muligheter og begrensninger.*" (In English: "One of the group? Inclusion and youth with sensory impairments – possibilities and limitations"). Rapport 2014 Mangfold og inkludering. Trondheim: NTNU samfunnsforskning AS.

King, G., et al. (2006) "Predictors of the leisure and recreation participation of children with physical disabilities: A structural equation modeling analysis." *Children's Health Care* 35(3): 209–234.

King, G., Law, M., Hurley, P., Petrenchik, T. and Schwellnus, H. (March 2010) "A developmental comparison of the out-of-school recreation and leisure activity participation of boys and girls with and without physical disabilities." *International Journal of Disability, Development and Education* 57(1): 77–107.

King, G., Law, M., King, S., Hurley, P., Hanna, S. and Kertoy, M. (2004) *Children's assessment of participation and enjoyment (PAC)*. San Antonio, TX: Harcourt Assessment.

King, G., Law, M., King, S., Rosenbaum, P., Kertoy, M. K. and Young, N. L. (2003) "A conceptual model of the factors affecting the recreation and leisure participation of children with disabilities." *Physical & Occupational Therapy in Pediatrics* 23(1): 63–90.

Kissow, A.-M. and Singhammer, J. (2012) "Participation in physical activities and everyday life of people with disabilities." *European Journal of Adapted Physical Activity* 5(2): 65–81.

Kolle, E., Steene-Johannessen, J., Klasson-heggebo, L., Andersen, L. B. and Andersen, S. A. (2009) "A 5-yr change in Norwegian 9-yr-olds'objectively assessed physical activity level." *Medicine and Science in Sport and Exercise* 41(7): 1368–1373.

Lalvani, P. (2013) "Privilege, comprise, or social justice: Teachers' conceptualizations of inclusive education." *Disability & Society* 28(1): 14–27.

Latour, B. (1987) *Science in action*. Cambridge: Harvard University Press.

Latour, B. (1992) "Where are the missing masses? The sociology of a few mundane artifacts" in W. E. Bijker and John Law (eds.) *Shaping technology/building society*, pp. 205–224. Cambridge: MIT Press.

Latour, B. (2002) *Aramis, or the love of technology*. Cambridge, MA: Harvard University Press.

Latour, B. (2008) *En ny sociologi for et nyt samfund Introduktion til Aktør-Netværk-teori* (in English: *A new sociology for a new society Introduction to Actor-network-theory*). København: Akademisk Forlag.

Lid, I. M. (2013) *Universell utforming. Verdigrunnlag, kunnskap og praksis* (In English: Universal Design. Basic values, knowledge and practice). Oslo: Cappelen Damm Akademisk.

Lid, I. M. (2014) "Universal design and disability: an interdisciplinary perspective." *Disability and Rehabilitation* 36(16): 1344–1349.

Lindsay, S. (2010) "Perceptions of health care workers prescribing augmentative and alternative communication devices to children." *Disability and Rehabilitation: Assistive Technology* 5(3): 209–222.

Litvak, S. and Enders, A. (2001) "The interface between individuals and environments" in G. L. Albrech and K. D. Seelman (eds.) *Handbook of disability studies*. Thousand Oaks, CA: Sage.

Livingstone, S. and Helsper, E. J. (2007) "Gradations in digital inclusion: Children, young people and the digital divide." *New Media & Society* 9(4): 671–696.

López, D. (2010) "The securitization of care spaces: lessons from Telecare," in M. Schillmeier and M. Domènech (eds.), New technologies and emerging spaces of care, pp. 39–55. Farnham: Ashgate.

Lupton, D. and Seymour, W. (2000) "Technology, selfhood and physical disability." *Social Science & Medicine* 50(12): 1851–1862.

MacKenzie, D. and Wajcman, J. (2005) "Introductory essay: The social shaping of technology" in D. Mackenzie and J. Wajcman (eds.) *The social shaping of technology*, second edition, pp. 3–27. Berkshire: Open University Press.

Majnemer, A. (2009) "Promoting participation in leisure activities: Expanding role of pediatric therapists." *Physical & Occupational Therapy in Pediatrics* 29(1): 1–5.

Majnemer, A., Shevell, M., Law, M., Birnbaum, R., Chilingaryan, G., and Rosenbaum, P. (2008) "Participation and enjoyment of leisure activities in school-aged children with cerebral palsy." *Developmental Medicine and Child Neurology* 50(10): 751–758.

Markussen, E., Strømstad, M., Carlsten, T. C., Hausstätter, R., and Nordahl, T. (2007) *Inkluderende spesialundervisning?* (in English: *Inclusive special education?*). Report no. 19/2007. Oslo/Hamar: NIFU STEP and the University College of Hedmark.

McMillan, S. J. and Morrison, M. (2006) "Coming of age with the internet: A qualitative exploration of how the internet has become an integral part of young people's lives." *New Media & Society* 8(1): 73–95.

Ministry of Education (2008) *Kartlegging av fritidstilbudet til barn og unge med nedsatt funksjonsevne* (in English: *Mapping leisure activities for children and young people with disabilities*). Rambøll: Report 2008.

Moser, I. (2003) *Road traffic accidents: The ordering of subjects, bodies and disability*. Oslo Norway: Unipub.

Moser, I. (2006) "Sociotechnical practices and difference on the interference between disability, gender and class." *Science, Technology & Human Values* 31(5): 1–28.

Moser, I. and Law, J. (1998) *Making voices: Disability 002, technology and articulation*. Oslo: Center for Technology, Innovation and Culture.

Murchland, S. and Parkyn, H. (2010) "Using assistive technology for schoolwork: The experience of children with physical disabilities." *Disability and Rehabilitation: Assistive Technology* 5(6): 438–447.

Näslund, R. and Gardelli, Å. (2013) "'I know, I can, I will try': Youths and adults with intellectual disabilities in Sweden using information and communication technology in their everyday life." *Disability & Society* 28(1): 28–40.

Newman, J. and Vidler, E. (2006) "More than a matter of choice? Consumerism and the modernisation of health care" in L. Bauld, K. Clarke and T. Maltby (eds.) *Social policy review 18: Analysis and Debate in Social Policy*, pp. 101–120. Bristol: The Polity Press.

NHS Executive, Health Services Guidelines (2006) *Voucher Scheme*. Retrieved from Internet April 28, 2006 from http://wheelchairusers.org.uk/content/voucher.htm.

Nordic Cooperation on Disability (NSH) (2004) *Provision of assistive technology in the Nordic countries*. Solna, Sweden.

The Norwegian Labour and Welfare Administration (2014) Retrieved 29th of August 2016 from https://www.nav.no/no/Person/Hjelpemidler/Nyheter+hele+landet/Aktivitetshjelpe midler+til+personer+over+26+%C3%A5r.386331.cms

Nyquist, A. J. (2012) *Jeg kan delta Barn med funksjonsnedsettelser og deltakelse i fysisk aktivitet – en multimetodestudie i en habiliteringskontekst* (in English: *I can participate, Children with disabilities and participation in physical activity – A multimethodical study in a rehabilitation context*). PhD thesis, The Norwegian School of Sport Science.

Øien, I., Fallang, B. and Østensjø, S. (2015) "Everyday use of assistive technology devices at school settings." *Disability and Rehabilitation Assistive Technology* 11(8): 630–635. doi:10.3109/17483107.2014.1001449

Olaussen, I. (2010) *Disability, technology & politics: The entangled experience of being hard of hearing.* PhD thesis. Centre for Technology, Innovation and Culture (TIK), University of Oslo, Norway.

Oliver, M. (1990) *The politics of disablement*. London: Palgrave Macmillan.

Østensjø, S. (2005) *Functioning and disability in young children with cerebral palsy. A study of everyday activities and the influence of motor impairments and environmental factors*. PhD dissertation, The University College of Oslo and Akershus.

Østensjø, S., Carlberg, E. B. and Vøllestad, N. K. (2005) "The use and impact of assistive devices and other environmental modifications on everyday activities and care in young children with cerebral palsy." *Disability and Rehabilitation* 27(14): 849–861.

Oudshoorn, N. and Pinch, T. (eds.) (2003) *How users matter: The co-construction of users and technology*. Cambridge: MIT Press.

Oudshoorn, N., Saetnan, A. R. and Lie, M. (2002) "On gender and things: Reflections on an exhibition on gendered artifacts." *Women's Studies International Forum* 25(4): 471–483.

Pape, T. L. B., Kim, J. and Weiner, B. (2002) "The shaping of individual meanings assigned to assistive technology: A review of personal factors." *Disability and Rehabilitation* 24(1/2/3): 5–20.

Paterson, K. and Hughes, B. (2002) "Disabled bodies" in P. Hancock, B. Hughes, E. Jagger, K. Paterson, R. Russell, E. Tulle-Winton and M. Tyler (eds.) *The body, culture and society: An introduction*, pp. 29–44. Buckingham: Open university Press.

Peter, J. and Valkenburg, P. M. (2006) "Research Note: Individual Differences in Perceptions of Internet Communication." *European Journal of Communication* 21(2): 213–226.

Priestly, M. (2003) "'It's like your hair going grey,' or is it? Impairment, disability and the habitus of old age" in S. Riddel and N. Watson (eds.) *Disability, culture and identity*, pp 53–64. Edinburgh: Pearson Education Limited.

Prior, S. (2011) *Towards the full inclusion of people with severe speech and physical impairment in the design of augmentative and alternative communication software*. PhD thesis, University of Dundee, Dundee.

Pullin, G. (2009) *Design meets disability*. Cambridge: MIT Press.

Räsänen, P. (2008) "The aftermath of the ICT revolution? Media and communication technology preferences in Finland in 1999 and 2004." *New Media & Society* 10(2): 225–245.

Räsänen, P. and Kouvo, A. (2007) "Linked or divided by the web? Internet use and sociability in four European countries." *Information, Communication & Society* 10(2): 225–245.

Ratzka, A. (2003) *From patient to consumer: Direct payments for assistive technology for disabled people's self-determination*. Stockholm, Sweden: Independent Living Institute.

Ravneberg, B. (2009) "Identity politics by design – Users, markets and the public service provision for assistive technology in Norway." *Scandinavian Journal of Disability Research* 11(2): 101–115.

Ravneberg, B. (2012) "Usability and abandonment of assistive technology." *Journal of Assistive Technologies* 6(4): 259–269.

Rekkedal, A. M. (2012) "Assistive hearing technologies among students with hearing impairments: Factors that promote satisfaction." *Journal of Deaf Studies and Deaf Education Advance Access* (May): 499–517. doi:10.1093/deafed/ens023

Rekkedal, A. M. (2013) "Teachers' use of assistive listening devices in inclusive schools." *Scandinavian Journal of Disability Research*. doi:10.1080/15017419.2012.761152

Reyes, de los, P. and Mulinari, D. (2005) *Intersektionalitet kritiska reflektioner över (o) jämlikhetens landskap* (in English: *Intersectionality: Critical reflections on an unequal landscape*). Malmö: Liber.

Riddle, S. (2007) "A sociology of special education" in L. Florian (ed.) *The Sage handbook of special education*, pp. 34–45. London: Sage.

Rose, D. and Blume, S. (2003) "Citizen as users of technology: An exploratory study of vaccines and vaccination" in Nelly Oudshoorn and Trevor Pinch (eds.) *How users matter, the co-construction of users and technology*. Cambridge: MIT Press.

Samuels, G. M. and Ross-Sheriff, F. (2008) "Identity, oppression and power feminism and intersectionality theory." *Affilia: Journal of Women and Social Work* 23(1): 5–9.

Sapey, B., Stewart, J. and Donaldson, G. (2004) *The social implication of increases in wheelchair use*. Report. Dept. of Applied Social Science, Lancaster University.

Scherer, M. J. (2002) *Assistive technology: Matching device and consumer for successful rehabilitation*. Washington, DC: American Psychological Association.

Scherer, M. J. (2005) *Living in the state of stuck: How assistive technology impacts the lives of people with disabilities*. Northampton, MA: Brookline Books.

Schillmeier, M. (2010) *Rethinking disability: Bodies, senses and things*. London and New York: Routledge.

Schillmeier, M. and Domènech, M. (eds.) (2009) "New technologies and emerging spaces of care – An introduction" in *New technologies and emerging spaces of care*, pp. 117. Farnham: Ashgate.

Seim, S. and Opsahl, K. (2015) "Barns deltakelse i fritid" (in English: Childrens participation in leisure time) in B. Fallang, B. C. R. Olsen, K. Opsahl, S. Seim, O. S. Ulvik, I. Øien and S. Østensjø (eds.) *Barns deltakels i hverdagsliv og profesjonell praksis – en utfordkende tilnærming* (in English: *Childrens participation in everyday life and profesional practice – An explorative approach*), pp. 183–202. Oslo: Universitetsforlaget.

Seippel, Ø., Abebe, D. and Strandbu, Å. (2012) *Å trene, trener, har trent? En longitudinell undersøkelse av sammenhengen mellom treningsvaner i tenårene og tidlig voksen alder* (in English: *To exercise, exercise, have exercised? A longitudinal investigation of the relationship between teenagers' exercise habits and early adulthood*). NOVA Report 12/2012.

Seymour, W. (2005) "ICTs and disability: Exploring the human dimensions of technological engagement." *Technology and Disability* 17: 195–204.

Seymour, W. and Lupton, D. (2004) "Holding the line online: Exploring wired relationships for people with disabilities." *Disability & Society* 19(4): 291–305.

Shakespeare, T. (2006) *Disability rights and wrongs*. London and New York: Routledge.

Shevlin, M., Kenny, M. and McNeela, C. (2002) "Curriculum access for pupils with disabilities: An Irish experience." *Disability & Society* 17(2): 159–169.

Shevlin, M., Winter, E. and Flynn, P. (2013) "Developing inclusive practice: Teacher perceptions of opportunities and constraints in the republic of Ireland." *International Journal of Inclusive Education* 17(10): 1119–1133.

Shikako-Thomas, K., Majnemer, A., Law, M. and Lach, L. (2008) "Determinants of participation in leisure activities in children and youth with cerebral palsy: Systematic review." *Physical and Occupational Therapy in Pediatrics* 28(2): 155–169.

Silverstone, R., Hirsch, E. and Morley, D. (1994) "Information and communication technologies and the moral economy of the household" in R. Silverstone and Eric Hirsch (eds.) *Consuming technologies: Media and information in domestic spaces*. London and New York: Routledge.

Skjølsvold, T. (2015) *Vitenskap, teknologi og samfunn. En introduksjon til STS* (in English: *Science, technology and society: An introduction to STS*). Oslo: cappelen Damm Akademisk.

Smith, D. H. (2013) "Deaf adults: Retrospective narratives of school experiences and teacher expectations." *Disability & Society* 28(5): 673–686.

Söderström, S. (2009) *Ungdom, teknologi og funksjonshemming: En studie av IKTs betydning i dagliglivet til ungdommer som har en funksjonsnedsettelse* (In English: *Youth, technology and disability: A study of the impact of ICT in daily life for young disabled people*). PhD thesis, NTNU.

Söderström, S. (2011) "Staying safe while on the move: Exploring differences in disabled and non-disabled young people's perceptions of the mobile phone's significance in daily life." *YOUNG Nordic Journal of Youth Research* 19(1): 91–109.

Söderström, S. (2012) "Disabled pupils' use of assistive ICT in Norwegian schools" in F. A. Auat Cheein (ed.) *Assistive technologies*, pp. 25–48. Kroatia: InTech.

Söderström, S. (2013) "Digital differentiation in young people's internet use – Eliminating or reproducing disability stereotypes." *Future Internet* 5: 190–204.

Söderström, S. and Ytterhus, B. (2010) "The use and non-use of assistive technologies from the world of information and communication technology by visually impaired young people: A walk on the tightrope of peer-inclusion." *Disability & Society* 25(3): 303–315.

Stirrat, M. J., Meyer, I. H., Oulette, S. C. and Gara, M. A. (2008) "Measuring identity and multiplicity and intersectionality: Hierarchical classes analysis (HICLAS) of sexual, racial, and gender identities." *Self and Identity* 7(1): 89–111.

Stone, D. A. (1984) *The disabled state*. Philadelphia: Temple University Press.

Strandbu, A. (2011) *Barnets deltakelse: hverdagslige og vanskelige beslutninger* (in English: *The child's participation: Everyday and difficult decisions*). Oslo: Universitetsforlaget.

Strandbu, Å. and Øia, T. (2007) *Ung i Norge. Skole, fritid og ungdomskultur* (in English: *Young in Norway: School, leisure and youth culture*). Oslo: Cappelen.

Svendsen, E. (2010) *"Tal her?" Formidling av avanserte kommunikasjonshjelpemidler og betjeningssystemer* (in English: *Speak here? Dissemination of advanced communication assistive tehnologies and operating systems*). Project report, NAV Sør-Trøndelag

Taub, D. E., Blinde, E. M. and Greer, K. R. (1999) "Stigma management through participation in sport and physical activity: Experiences of male college students with physical disabilities." *Human Relations* 52(11): 1469–1484.

Taub, D. E. and Greer, K. R. (2000) "Physical activity as normalizing experience for school-age children with physical disabilities." *Journal of Sport & Social Issues* 24(4): 395–414.

Telama, R., Yang, X., Hirvensalo, M. and Raitakari, O. (2006) "Participation in organized youth sport as a predictor of adult physical activity: A 21-year longitudinal study." *Pediatric Exercise Science* 17: 76–88.

Telama, R., Yang, X., Viikari, J., Välimäki, I., Wanne, O. and Raitakari, O. (2005) "Physical activity from childhood to adulthood. A 21-year tracking study." *American Journal of Preventive Medicine* 28(3): 267–273.

Tøssebro, J., Engan, E. and Ytterhus, B. (2006) "En inkluderende skole?" (In English: An inclusive school?) in J. Tøssebro and B. Ytterhus (eds.) *Funksjonshemmede barn i familie og skole – idealer og hverdagspraksis* (In English: *Disabled children in families and schools – Ideals and everyday practices*). Oslo: Gyldendal akademisk.

Tøssebro, J. and Lundeby, H. (2002) *Å vokse opp med funksjonshemming* (in English: To grow up with disability). Oslo: Gyldendal akademisk.

Tremain, S. (2005) *Foucault and the government of disability*. Ann Arbor: The University of Michigan Press.

Tronsmo, P. (2010) *Ledelse i utdanningssektoren* (in English: *Management in the education sector*). Bedre Skole 1:2010 (in English: Better Schools 1:2010).

Tulle-Winton, E. (2002) "Old bodies," in P. Hancock, B. Hughes, E. Jagger, K. Paterson, R, Russell, E. Tulle-Winton and M. Tyler (eds.), *The body, culture and society: An introduction*, pp. 64–83. Buckingham: Open University Press.

110   Bibliography

UNESCO. (1994) *The Salamanca statement and framework for action on special needs education.* Paris: UNESCO.

United Nations. (2008) *Convention on the rights of persons with disabilities.* New York: UN.

Vaage, O. F. (2008) *Norsk mediebarometer 2007* (in English: *Norwegian media barometer 2007*). Oslo: Statistisk Sentralbyrå.

Vicente, M. R. and Lòpez, A. J. (2010) "A multidimensional analysis of the disability digital divide: Some evidence for internet use." *The Information Society* 26: 48–64.

Walker, A. and Foster, L. (2013) "Active ageing: Rhetoric, theory and practice" in R. Ervik and T. S. Lindén (eds.) *The making of ageing policy: Theory and practice in Europe,* pp. 27–52. Cheltenham: Edward Elgar Publishing.

Watson, N. (2002) "Well, I know this is going to sound very strange to you, but I don't see myself as a disabled person: Identity and disability." *Disability and Society* 17(5): 509–527.

Wendelborg, C. (2010) *Barrierer mot deltakelse. Familier med barn og unge med nedsatt funksjonsevne* (in English: *Barrier to participation: Families with children and youth with impairments*). Trondheim: NTNU Samfunnsforskning.

Wendelborg, C. (2014) "Fra barnehage til videregående skole – veien ut av jevnaldermiljøet" (in English: From kindergarten to highschool – The road out of the peergroup milieu) in J. Tøssebro and C. Wendelborg (eds.) *Oppvekst med funksjonshemming. Familie, livsløp og overganger* (in English: *Growing up with disabilities: Family, life cycle and transitions*), pp. 35–58. Oslo: Gyldendal Akademisk.

Wendelborg, C. and Kvello, Ø. (2010) "Perceived social acceptance and peer intimacy among children with disabilities in regular schools in Norway." *Journal of Applied Research in Intellectual Disabilities* 23(2): 143–153.

Wendelborg, C. and Tøssebro, J. (2010) "Marginalisation processes in inclusive education in Norway – A longitudinal study of classroom participation." *Disability & Society* 25(6): 701–714.

Wendell, S. (1996) *The rejected body: Feminist philosophical reflections on disability.* New York: Routledge.

WHO. (2007) *International classification of functioning, disability and health: Children and youth version,* p. 9. Geneva: WHO Press.

Wielandt, T., McKenna, K., Tooth, L. and Strong, J. (2006) "Factors that predict the post-charge use of recommended assistive technology (AT)." *Disability & Rehabilitation: Assistive Technology* 1(1–2): 29–40.

Wik, S. E. and Tøssebro, J. (2013) *Unge funksjonshemmede i møte med NAV: Ett år med arbeidsavklaring* (in English: *Young disabled people meeting with NAV: One year with work assessment*). Report 2013. Trondheim: NTNU Samfunnsforskning.

Wilhite, B., Martin, D. and Shank, J. (2016) "Facilitating physical activity among adults with disabilities." *Therapeutic Recreation Journal* 50(1): 33–54.

Wilson, J. (2002) "Communications artefacts: The design of objects and the object of design" in Frascara Jorge (ed.) *Design and the social sciences: Making connections,* pp. 24–32. London: Taylor & Francis.

Winance, M. (2006) "Trying out the wheelchair: The mutual shaping of people and devices through adjustment." *Science, Technology & Human Values* 31(1): 52–72.

Winance, M. (2014) "Universal design and the challenge of diversity, reflections on the principles of UD, based on empirical research of people's mobility." *Disability & Rehabilitation* 36(16): 1334–1343.

Witsø, A. E. (2013) *Participation in older adults – In the context of receiving home-based services.* Doctoral thesis, NTNU, Trondheim.

Woods, B. and Watson, N. (2004a) "The social and technological history of wheelchairs." *International Journal of Therapy and Rehabilitation*, 11(9): 407–410.

Woods, B. and Watson, N. (2004b) *Wheelchairs as political machines.* Paper presented at the Healthy Innovation Workshop, University of Manchester, 8–10 July 2004.

Ytterhus, B., Egilson, S. T., Traustadóttir, R. and Berg, B. (2015) "Perspectives on Child-hood and Disability" in R. Traustaddóttir, B. Ytterhus, S. T. Egilson and B. Berg (eds.) *Childhood and disability in the nordic countires being, becoming, belonging*, pp. 15–33. New York: Palgrave Macmillan.

Yu, L. (2006) "Understanding information inequality: Making sense of the literature of the information and digital divides." *Journal of Liberianship and Information Science* 38(4): 229–252.

Index